SNAKE

Coloring Book for Adults

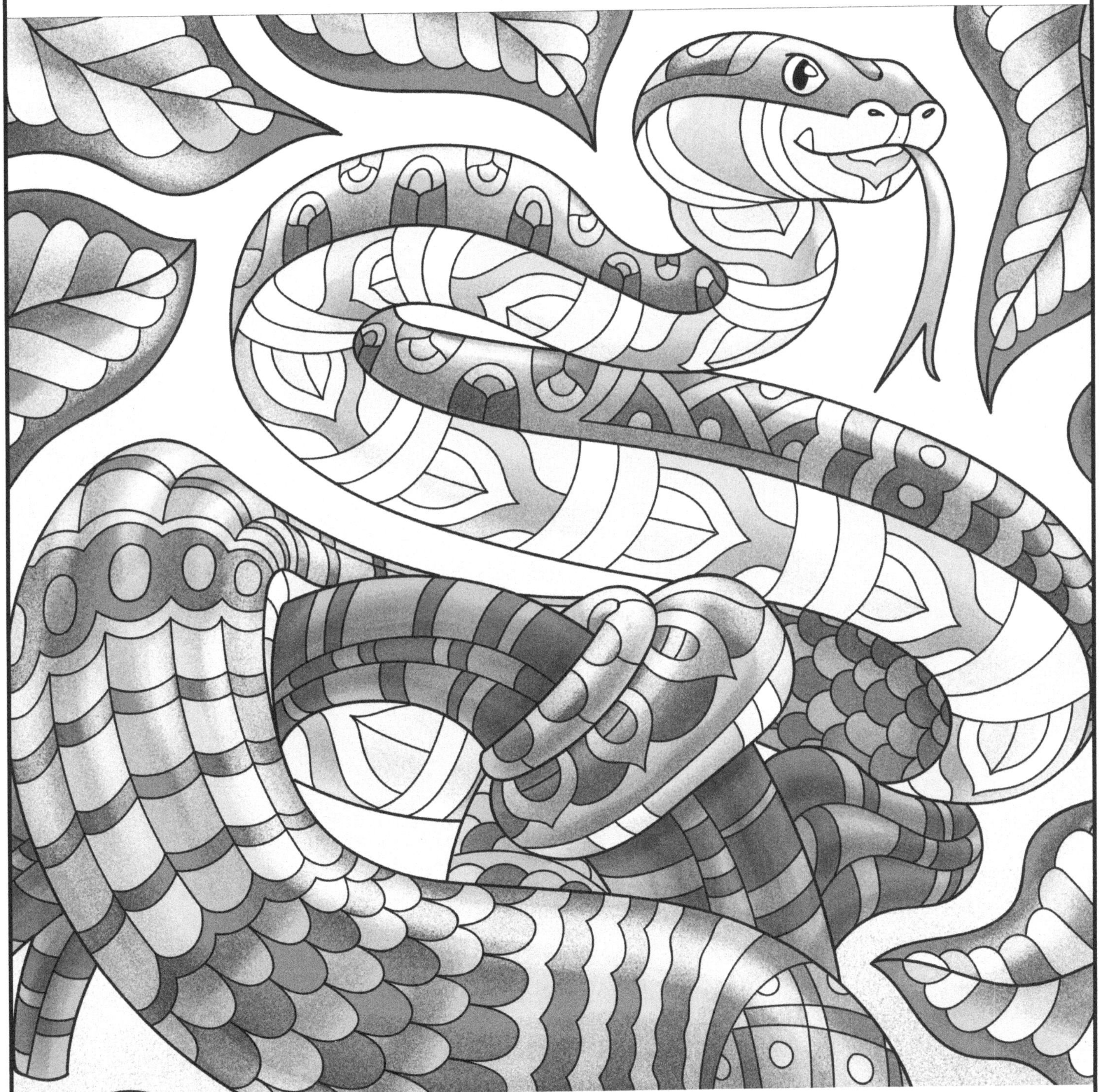

Dylanna Press

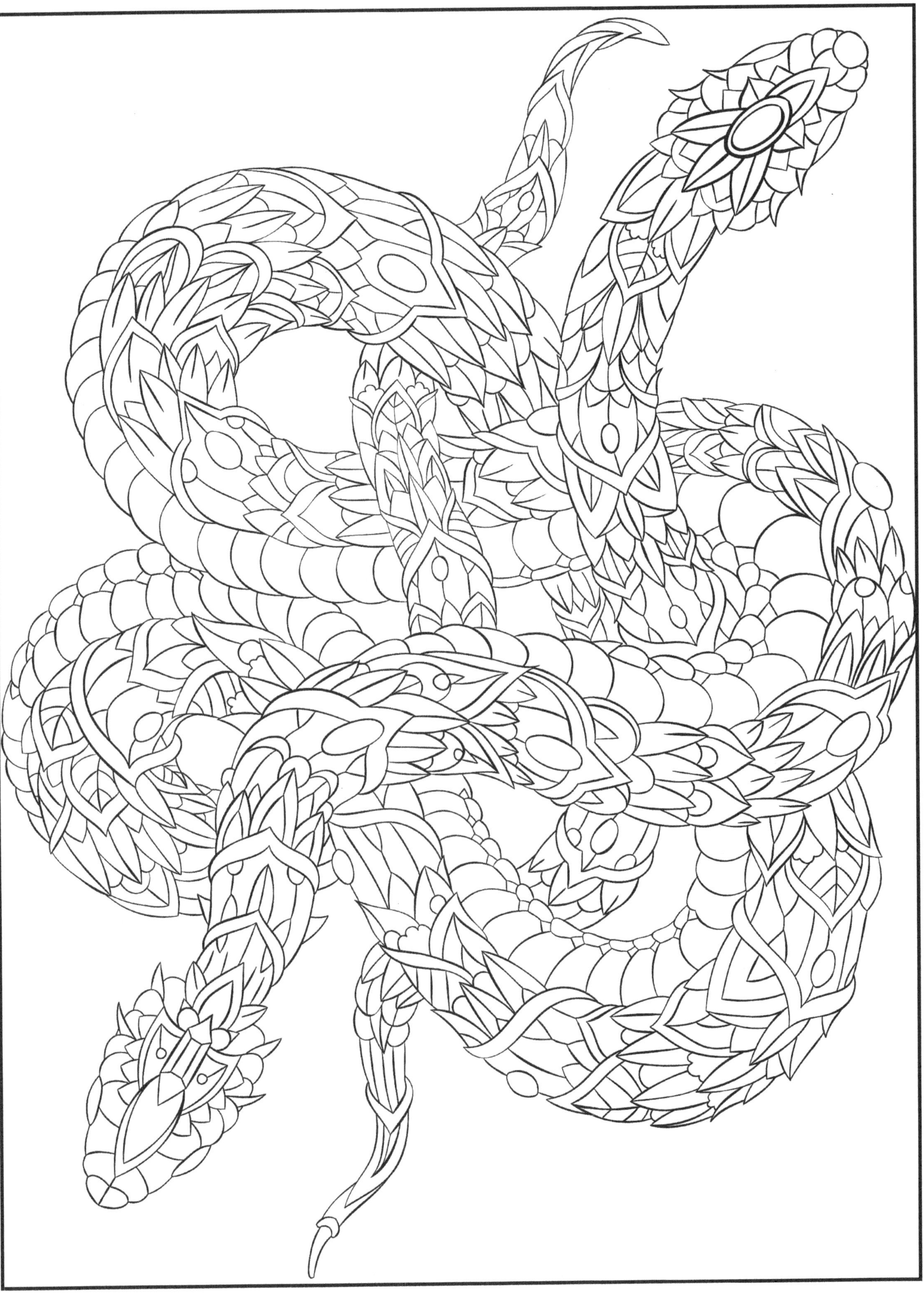

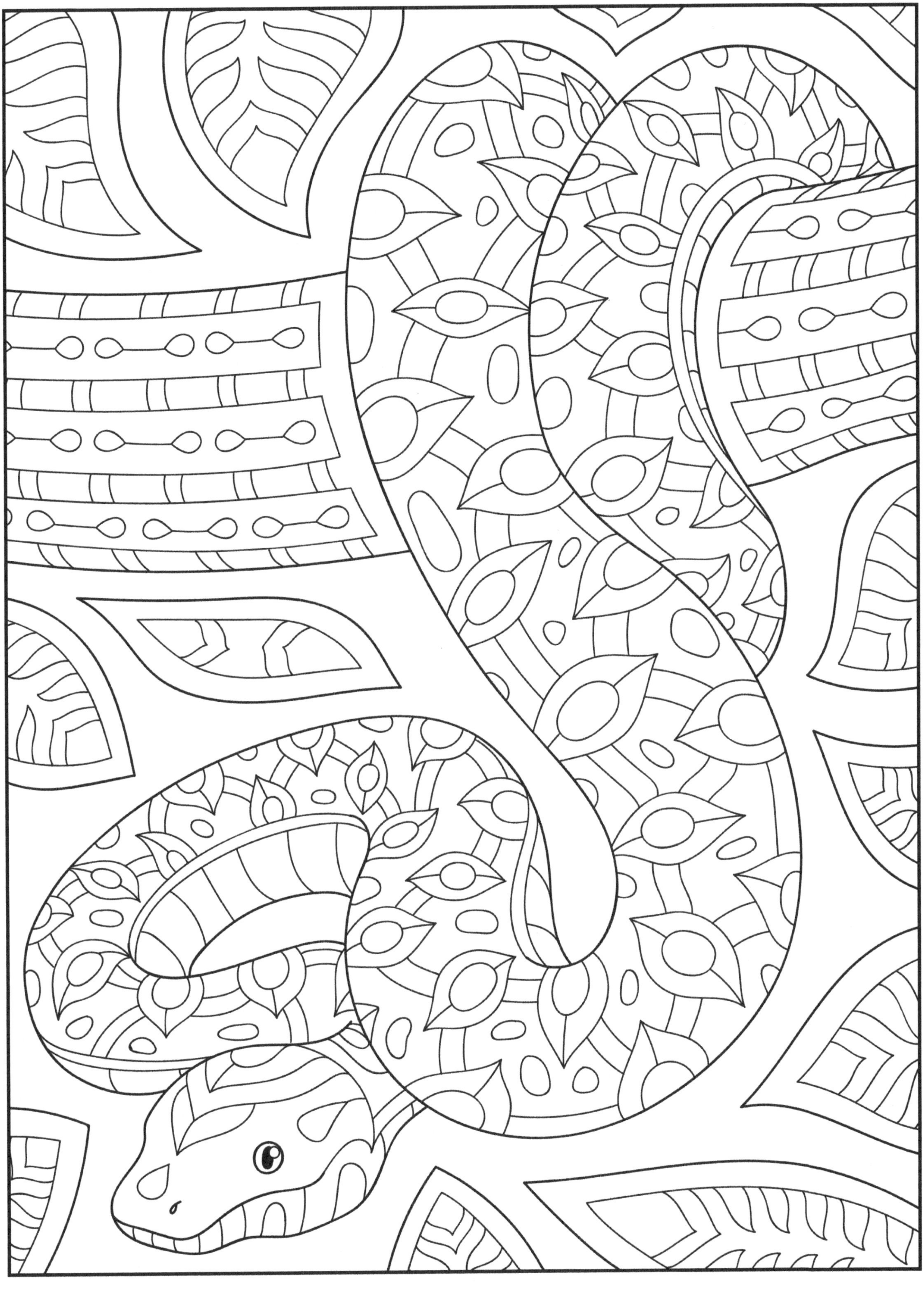

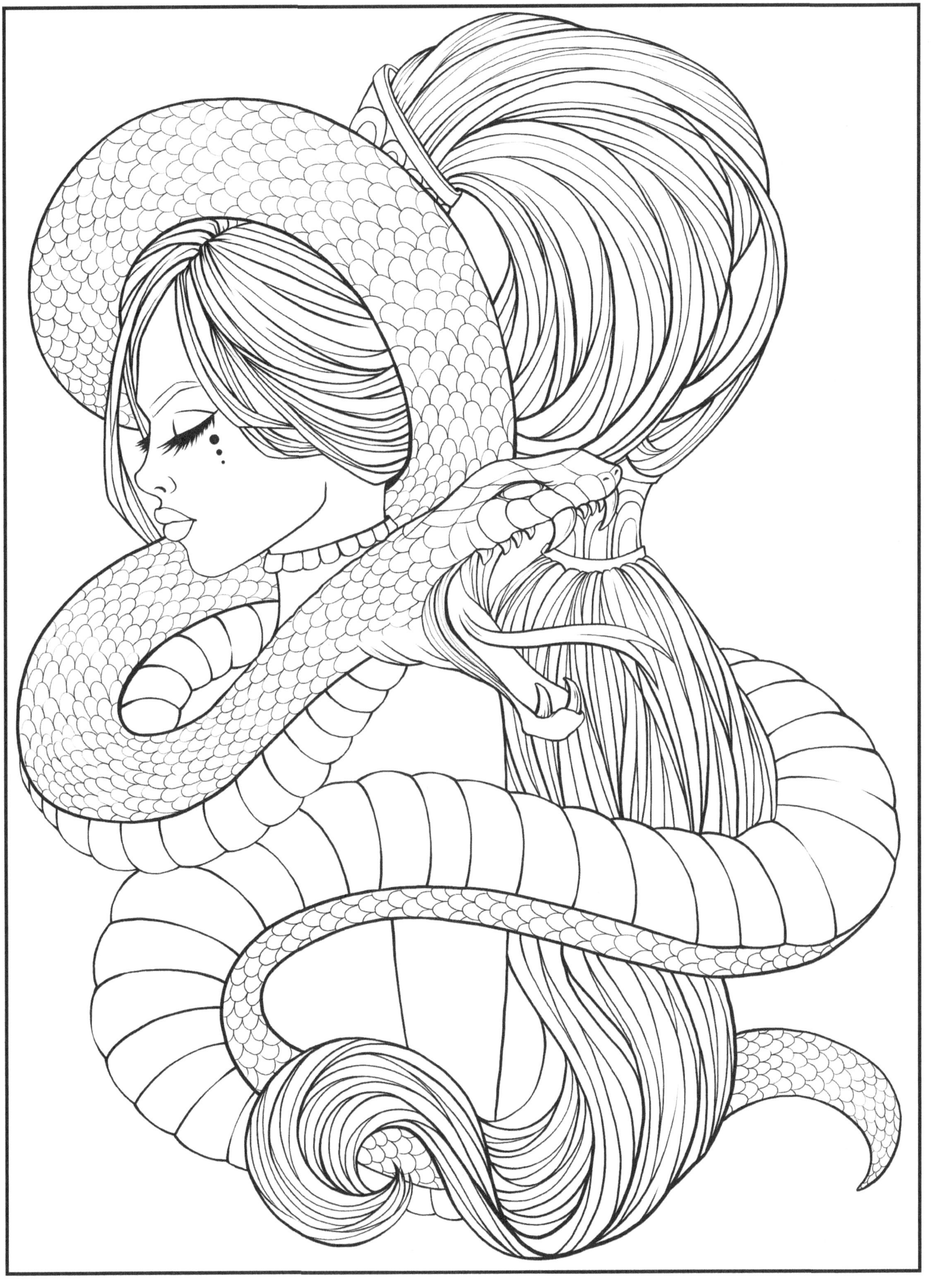

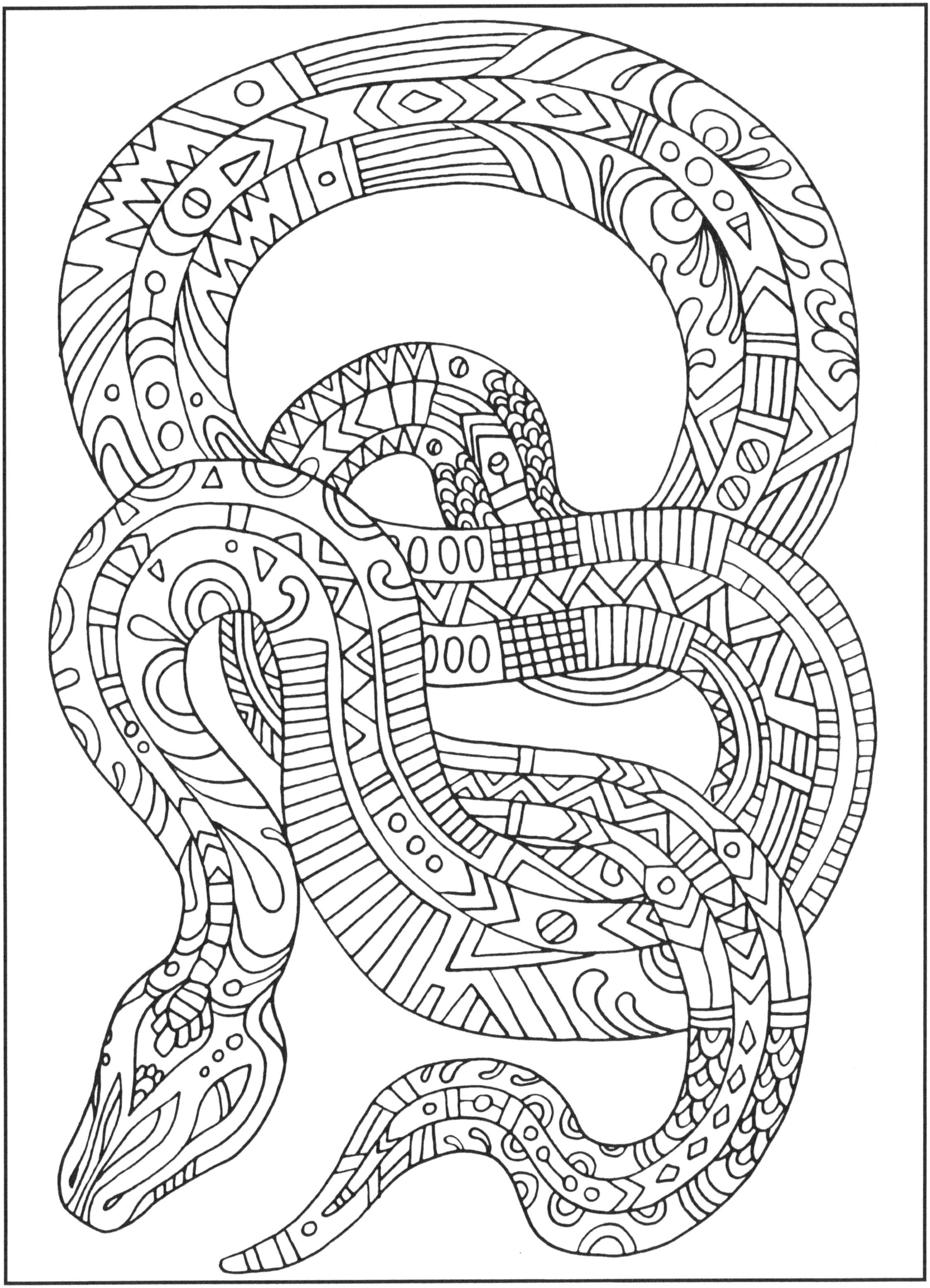

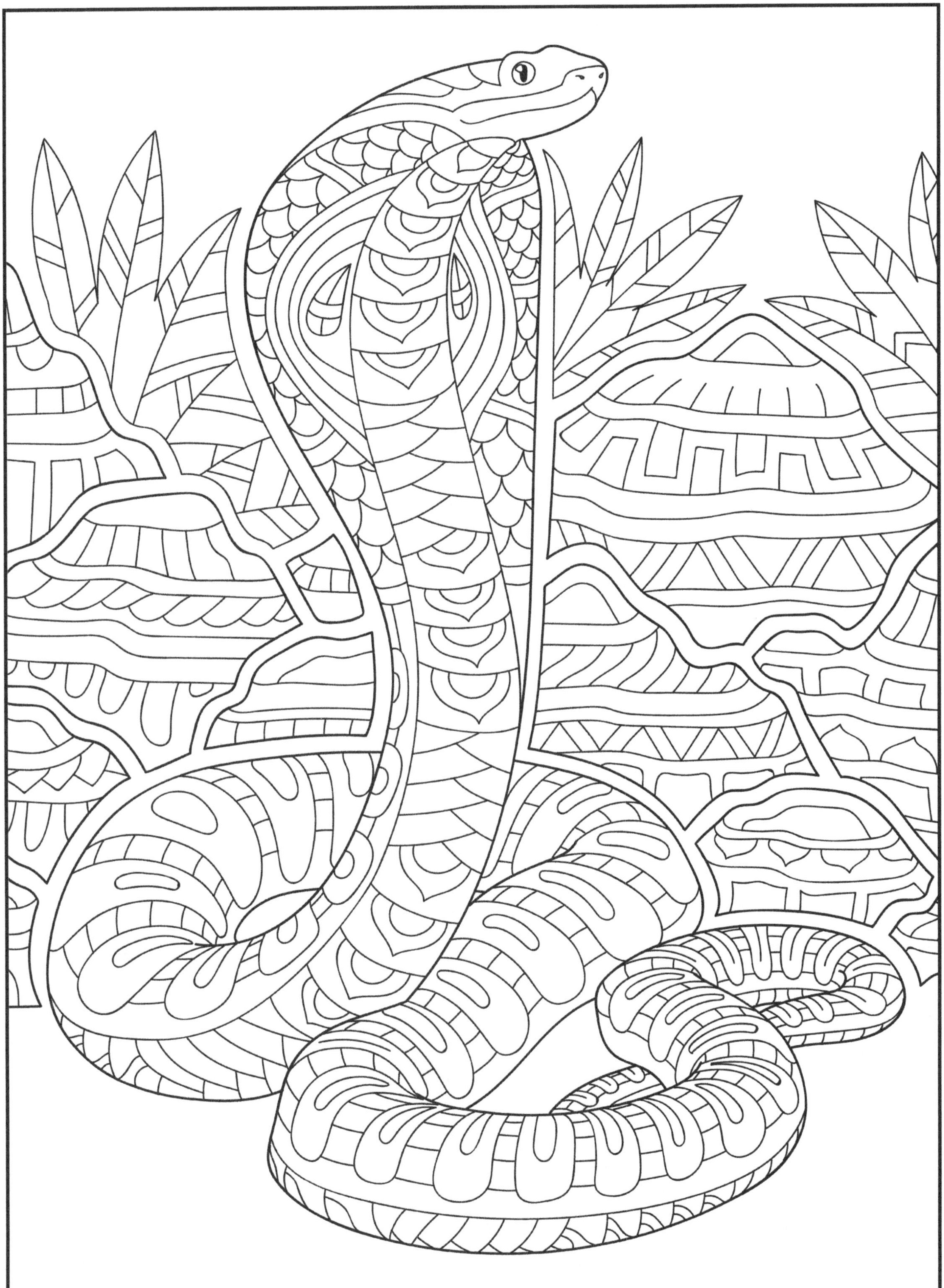

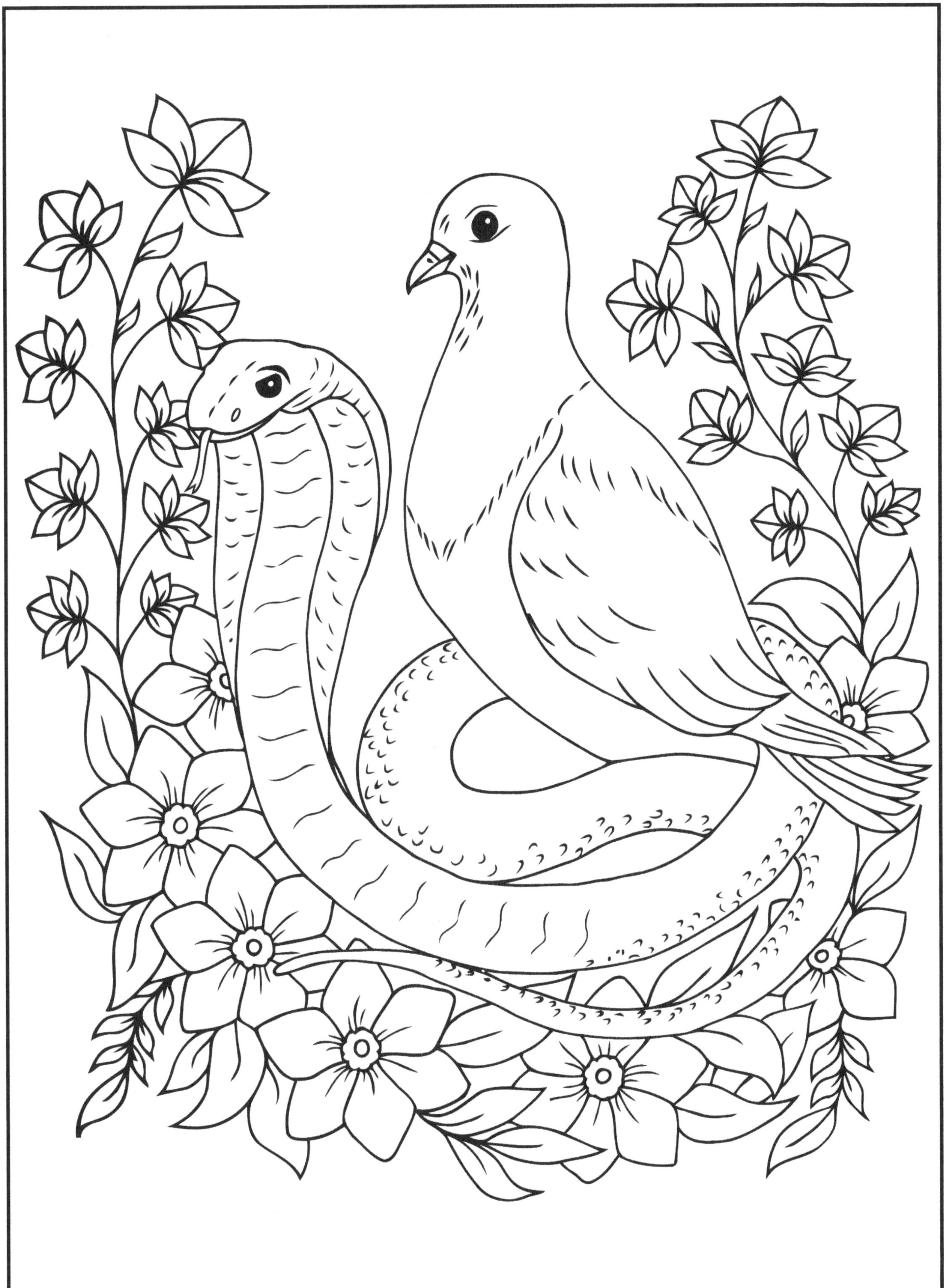

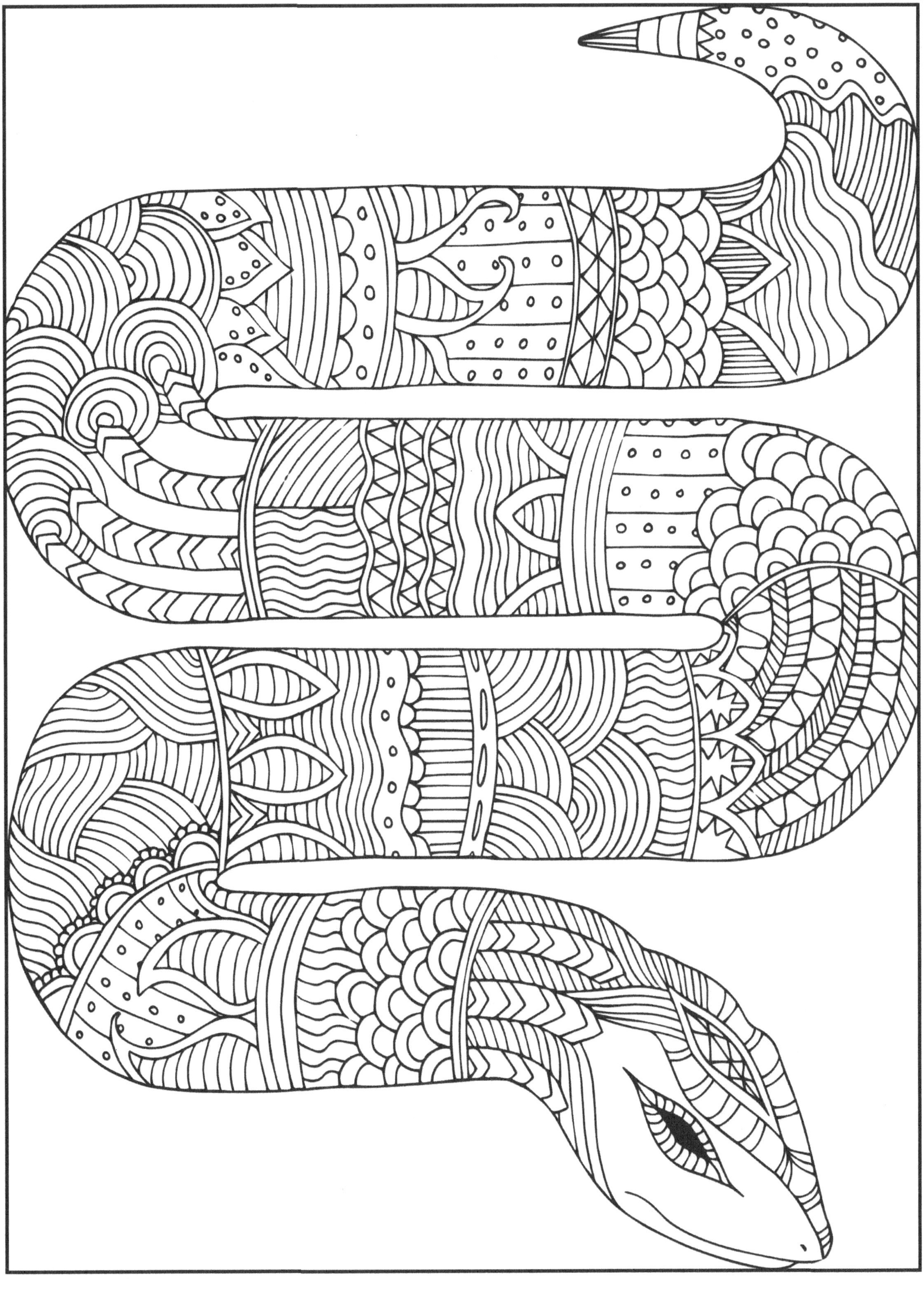

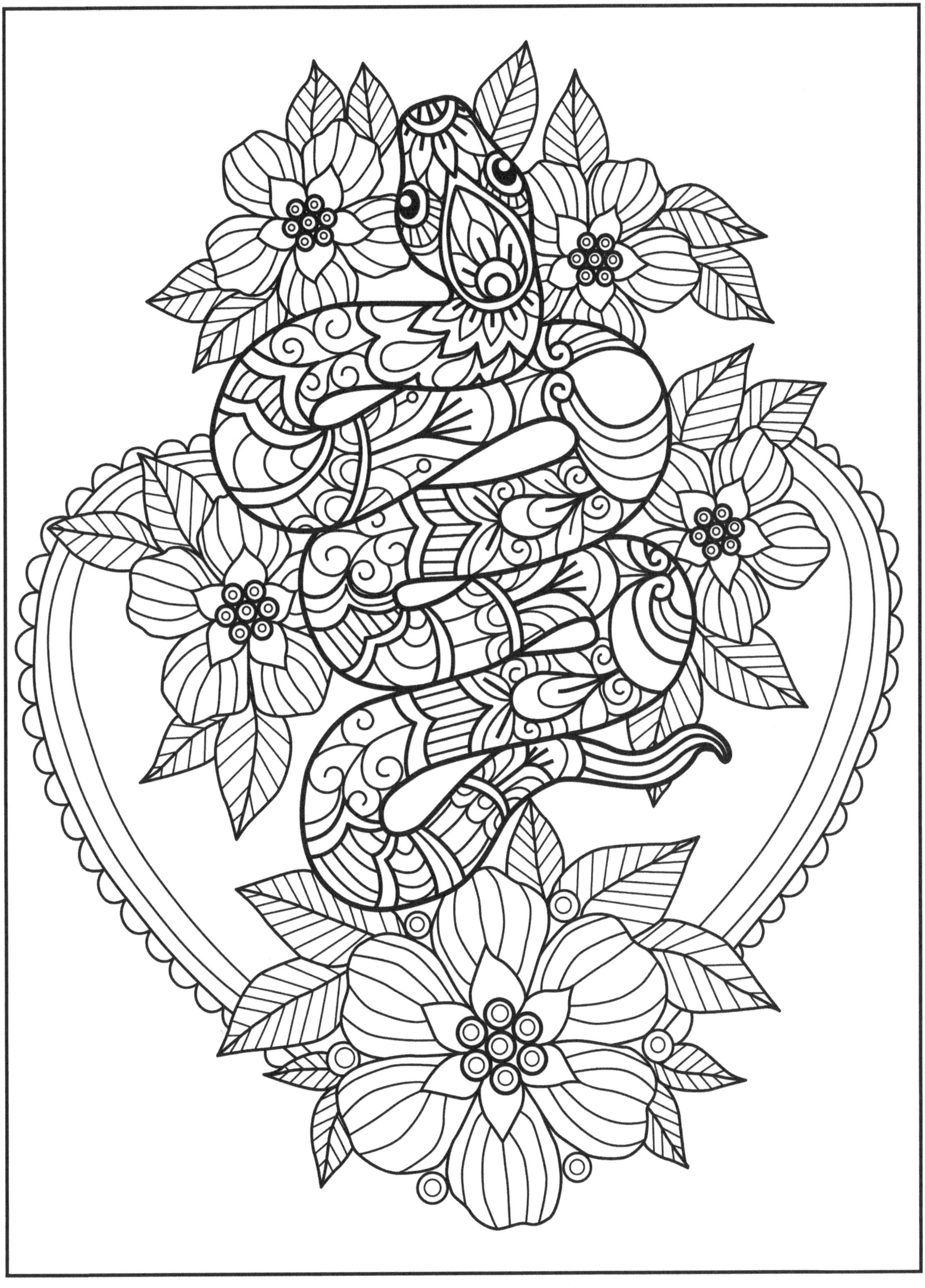

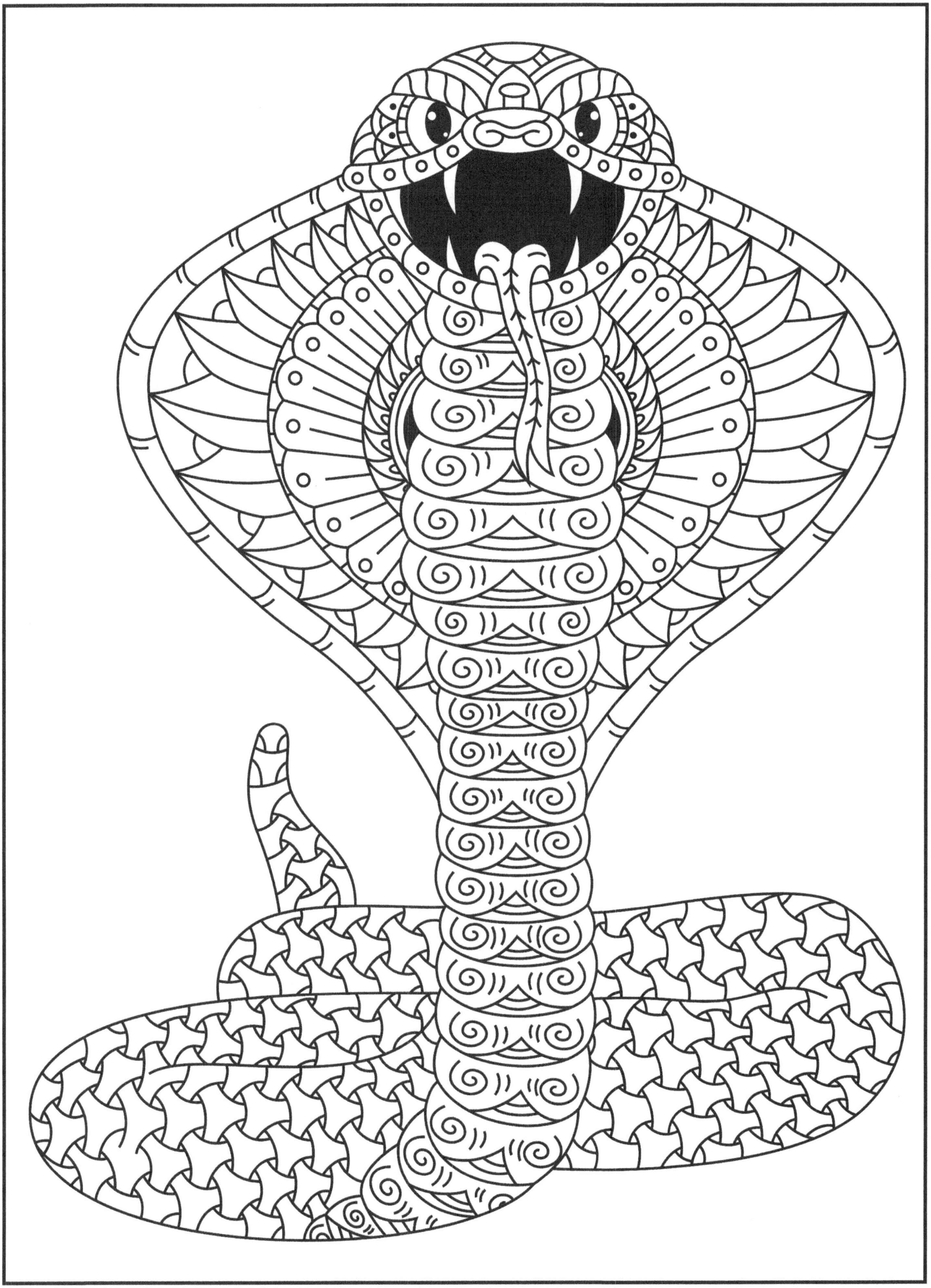

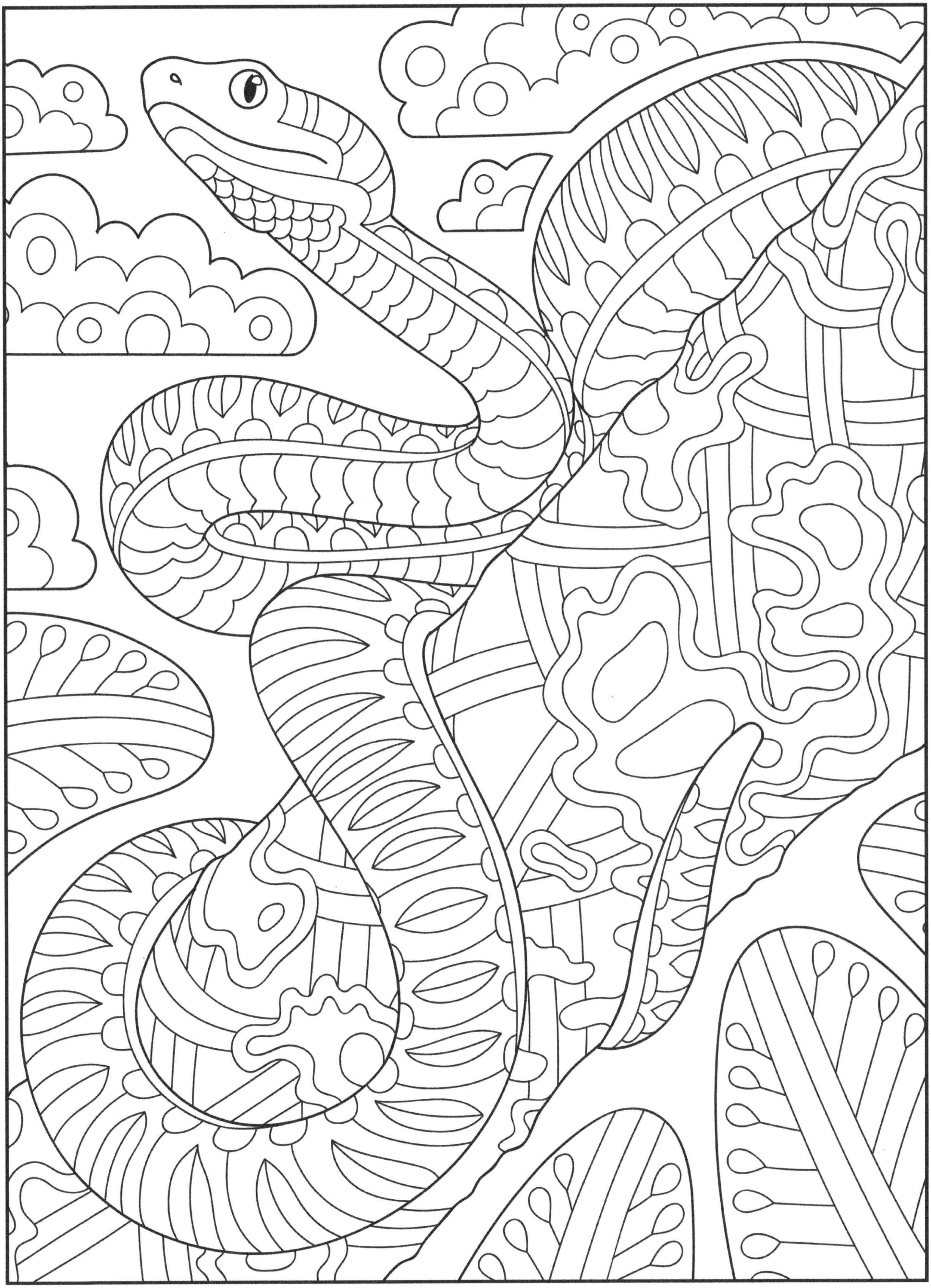

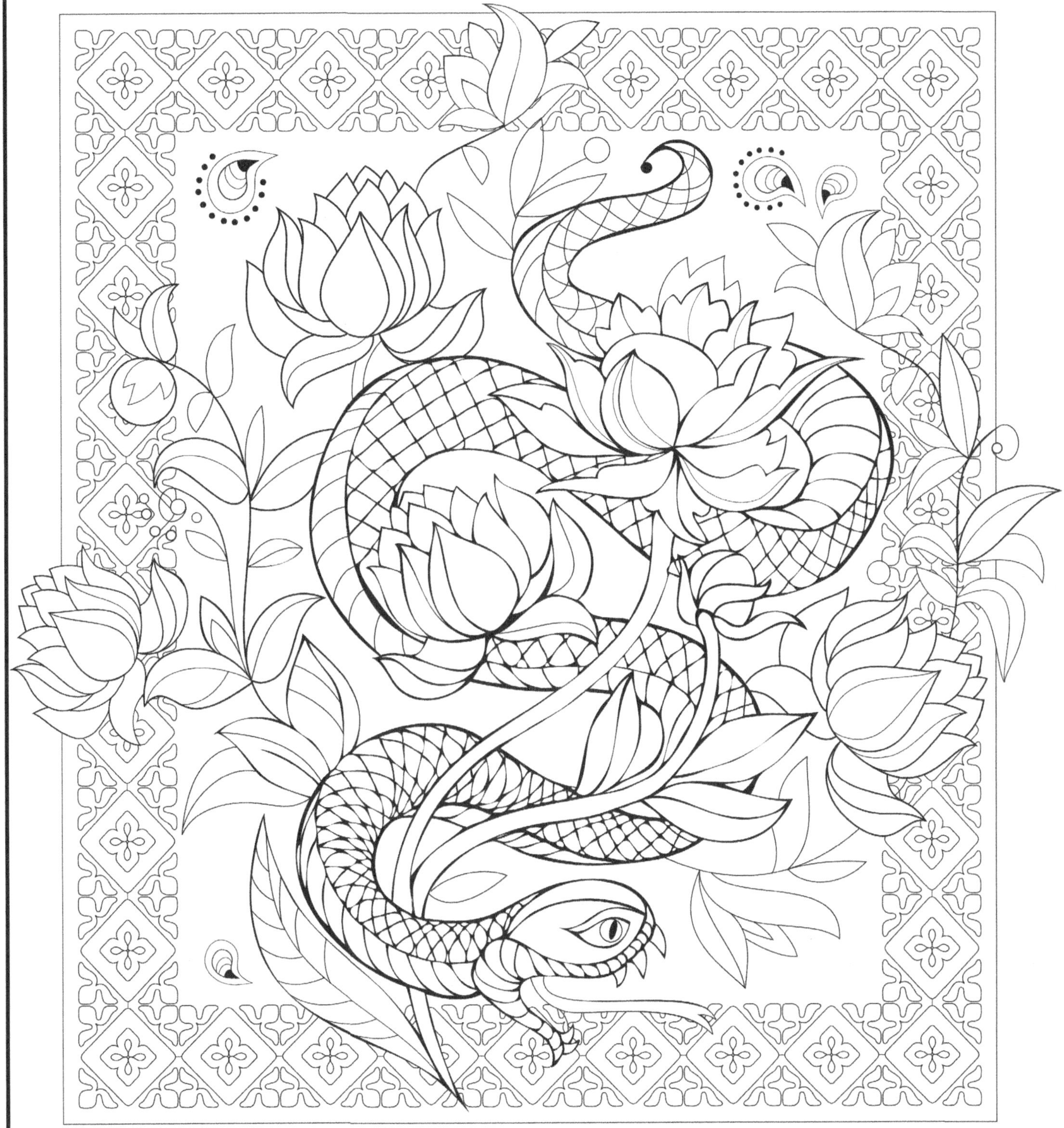

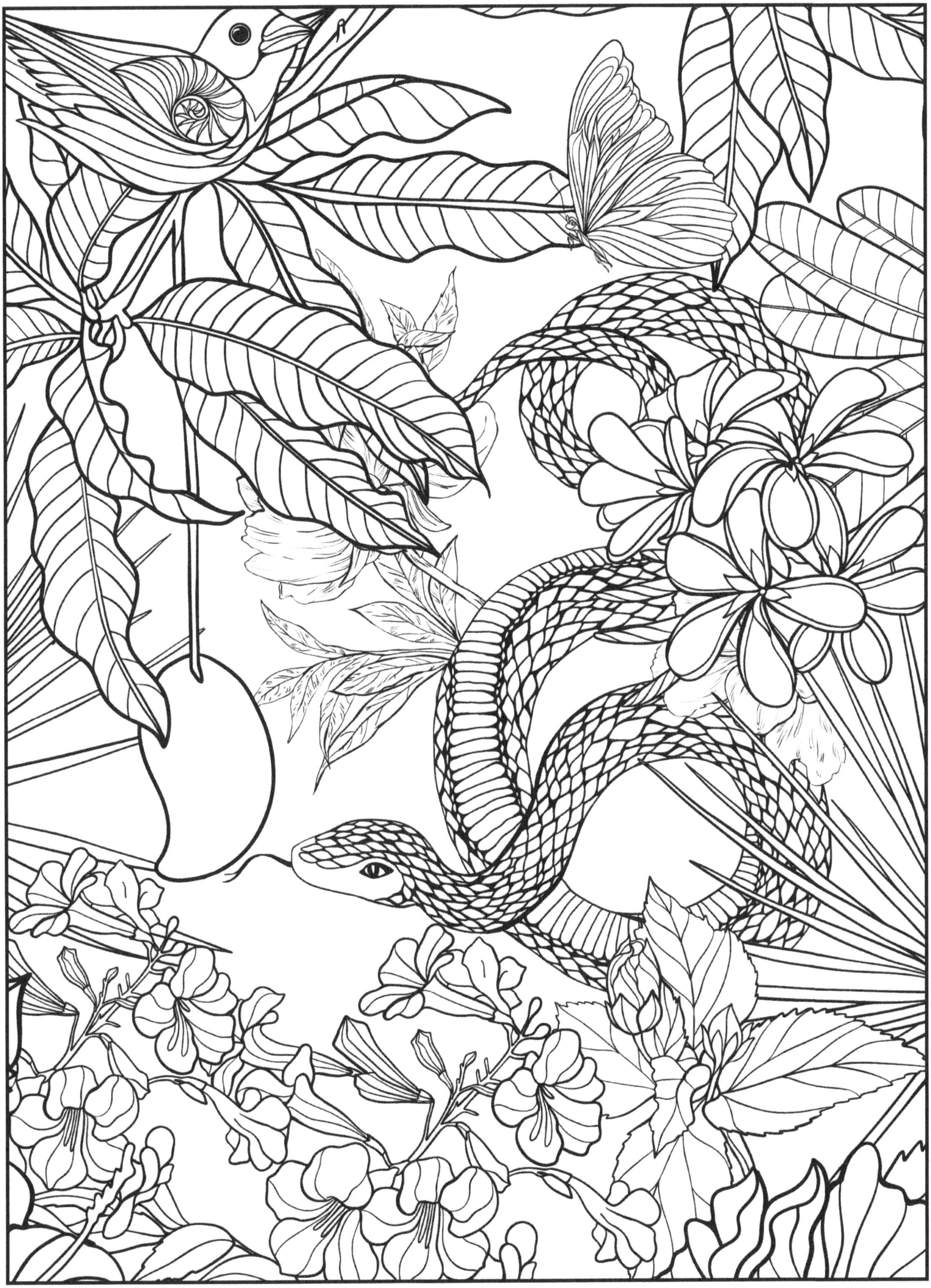

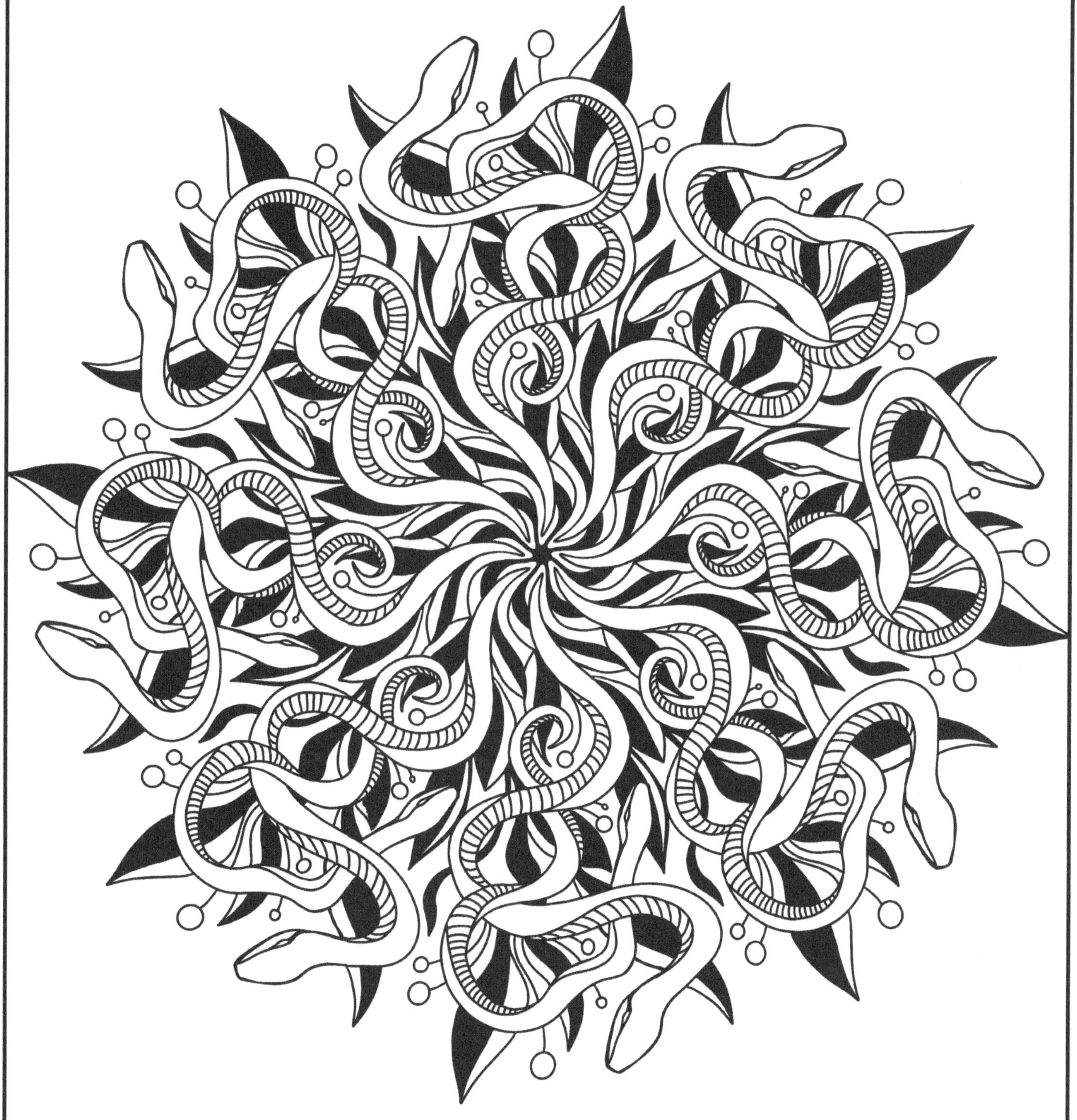

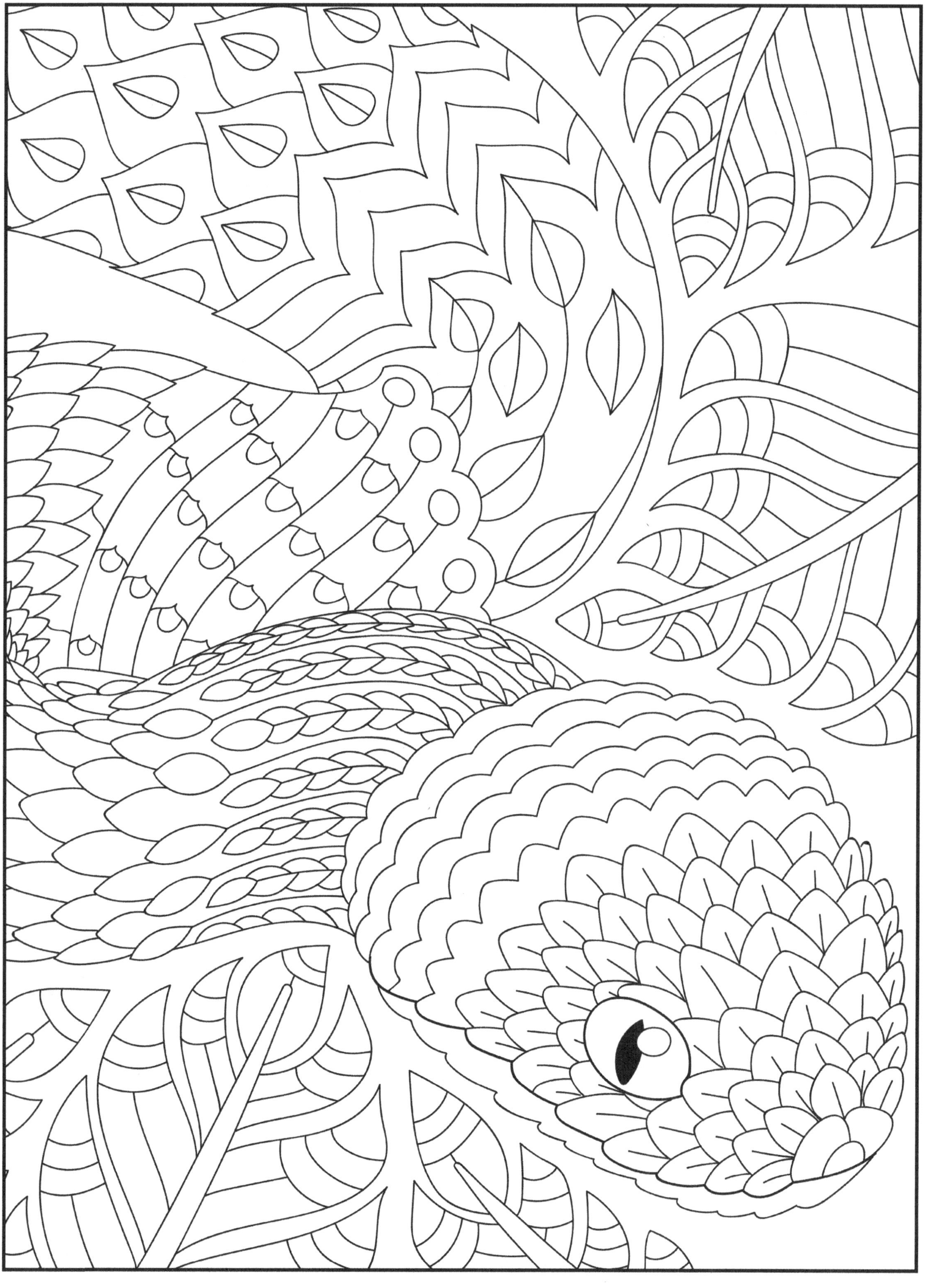

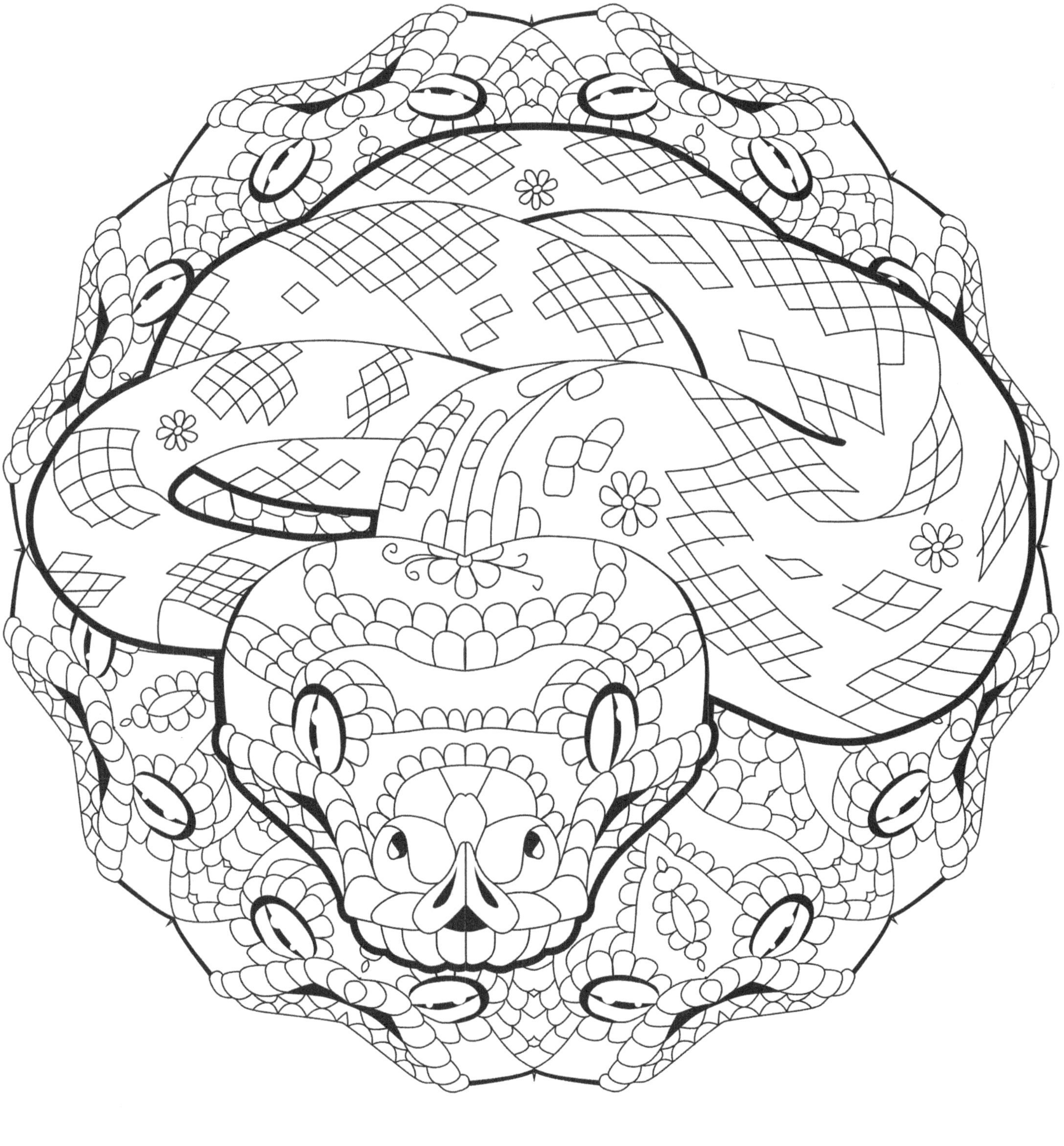

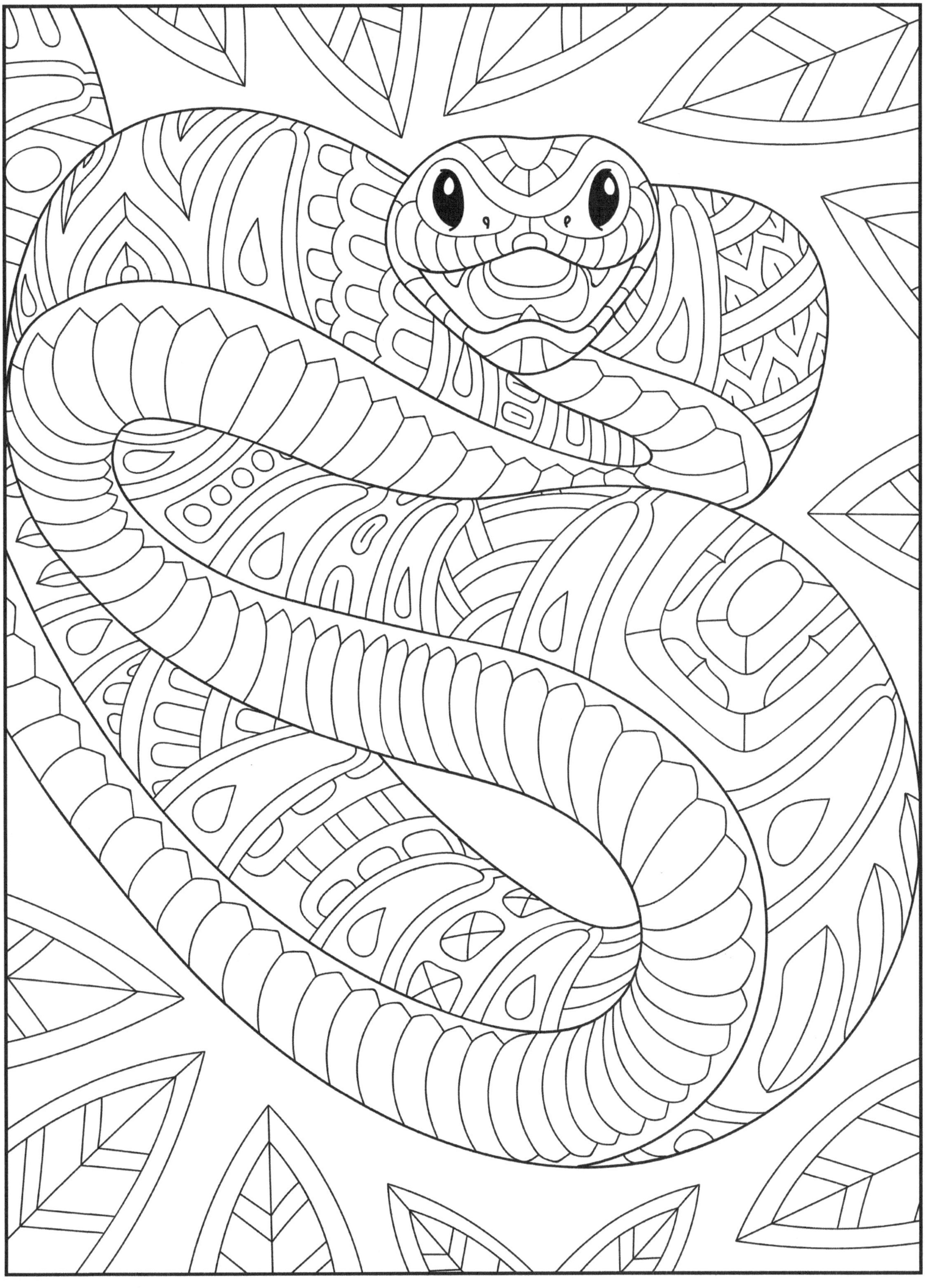

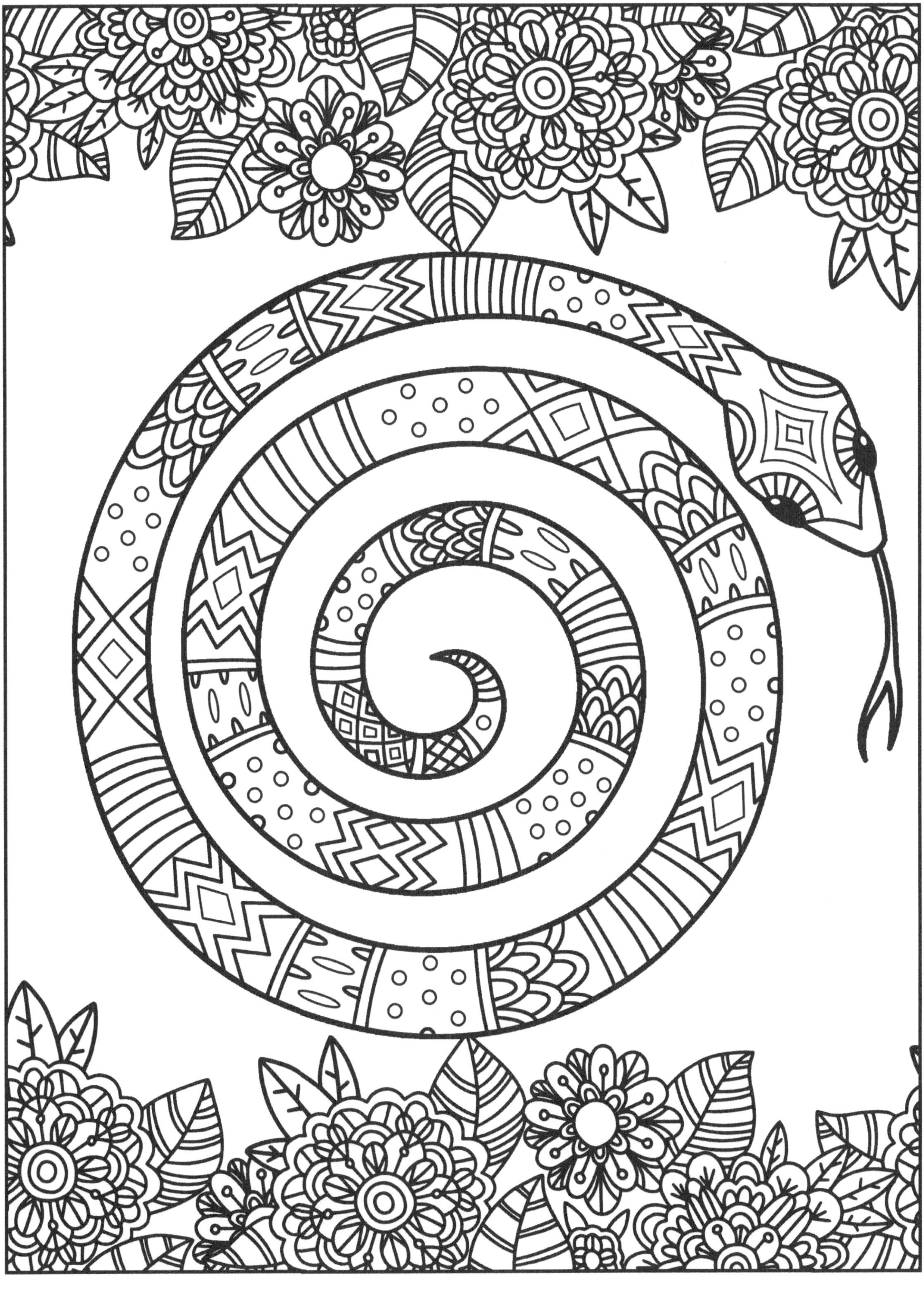

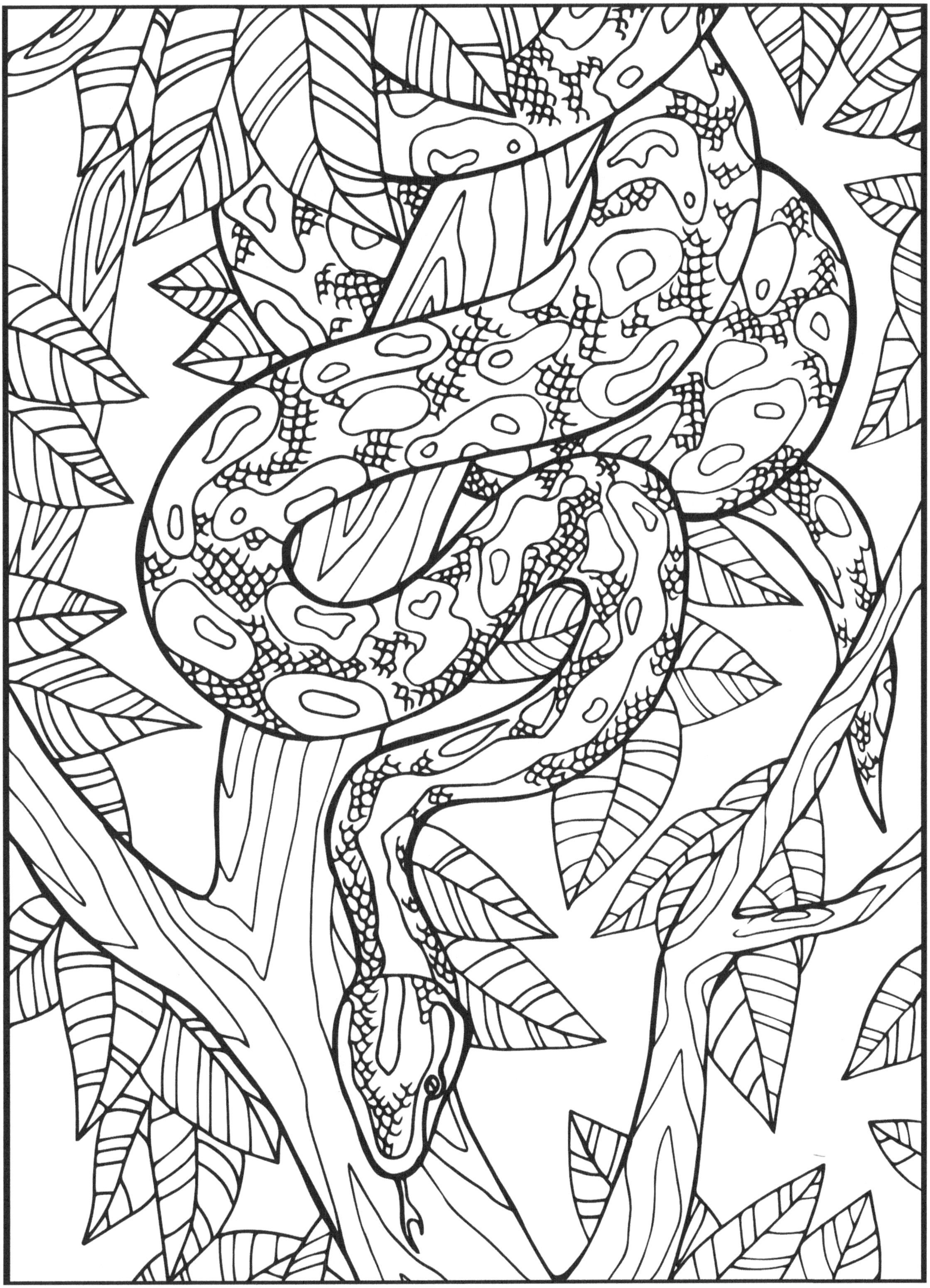

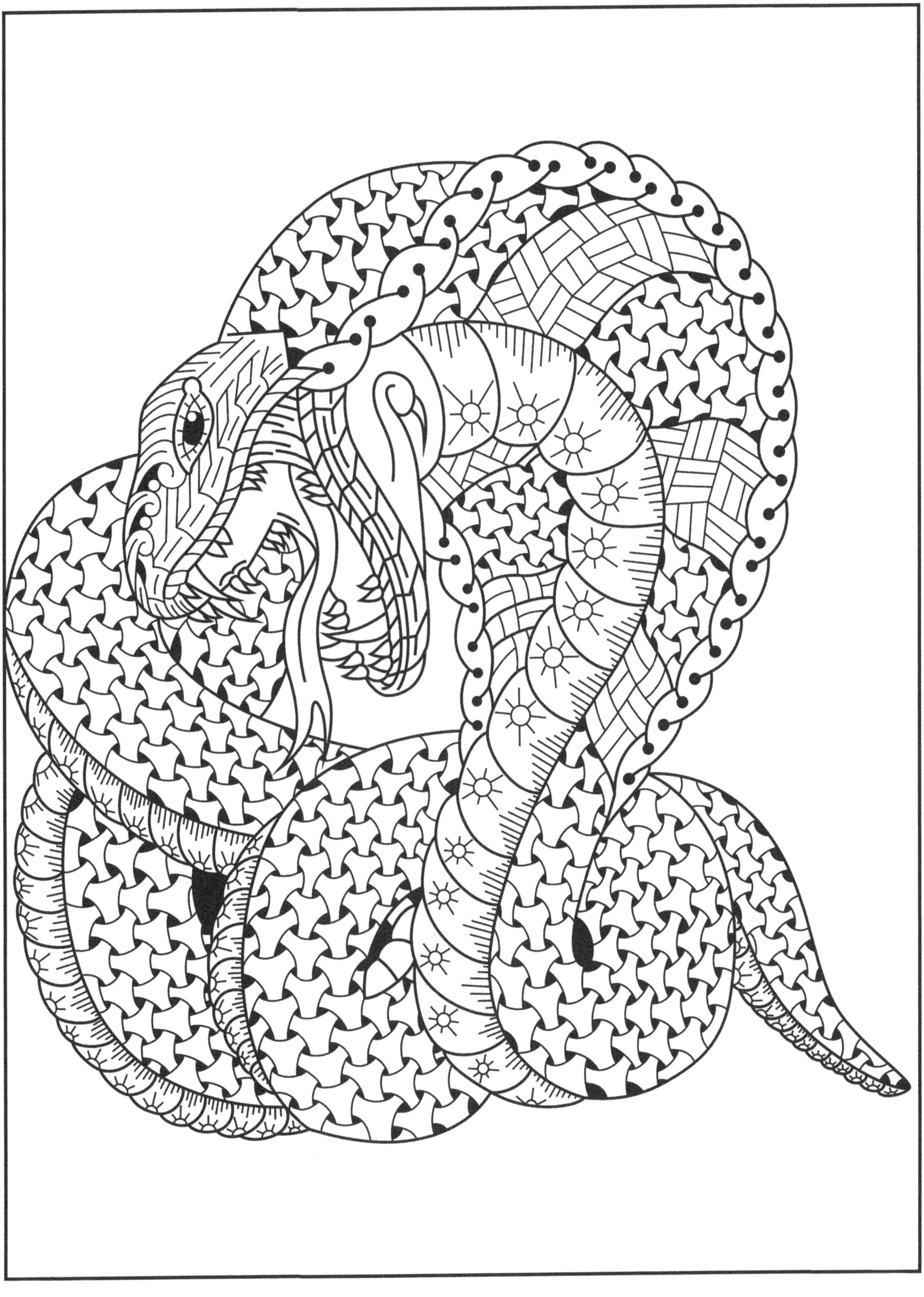

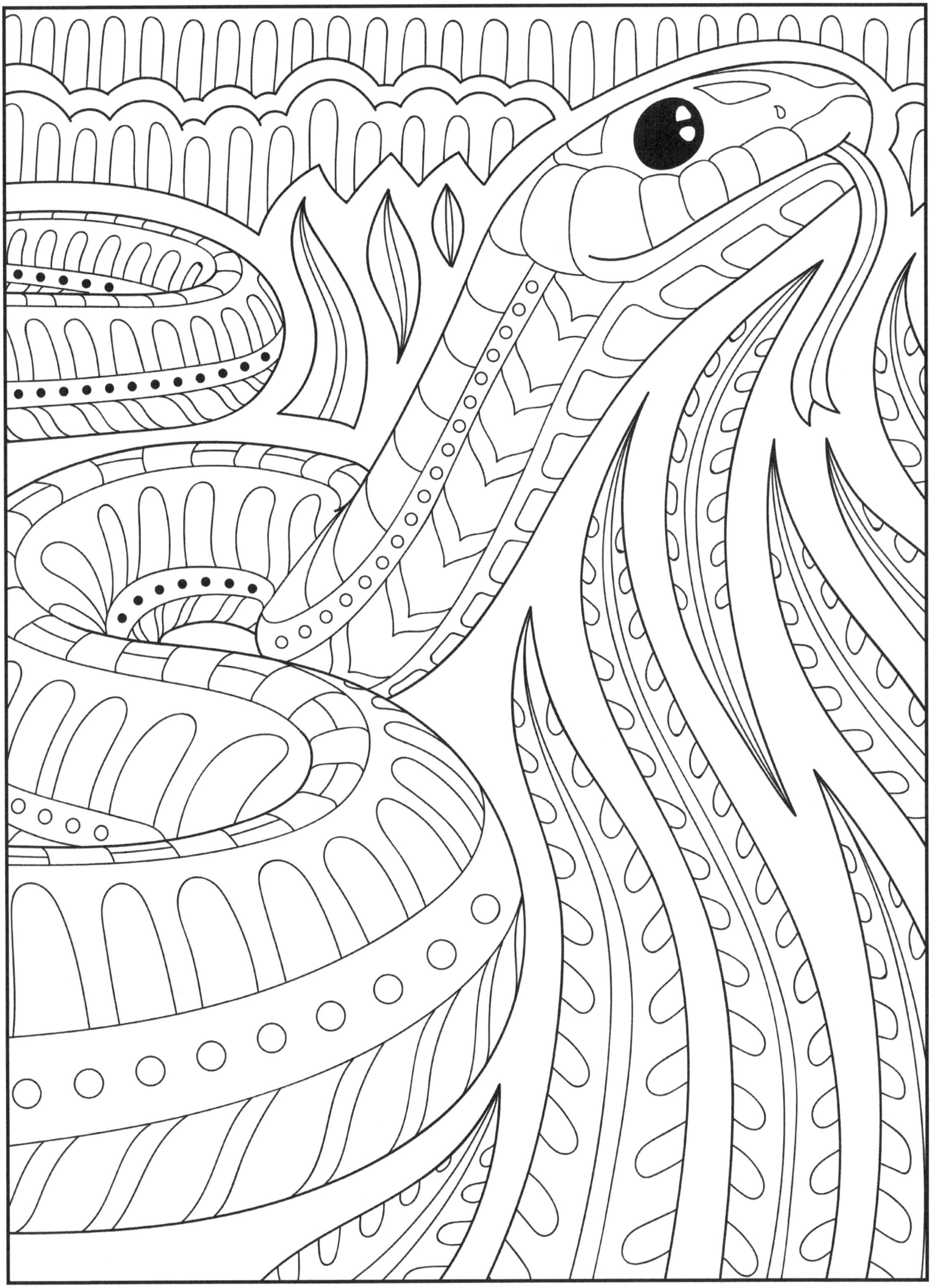

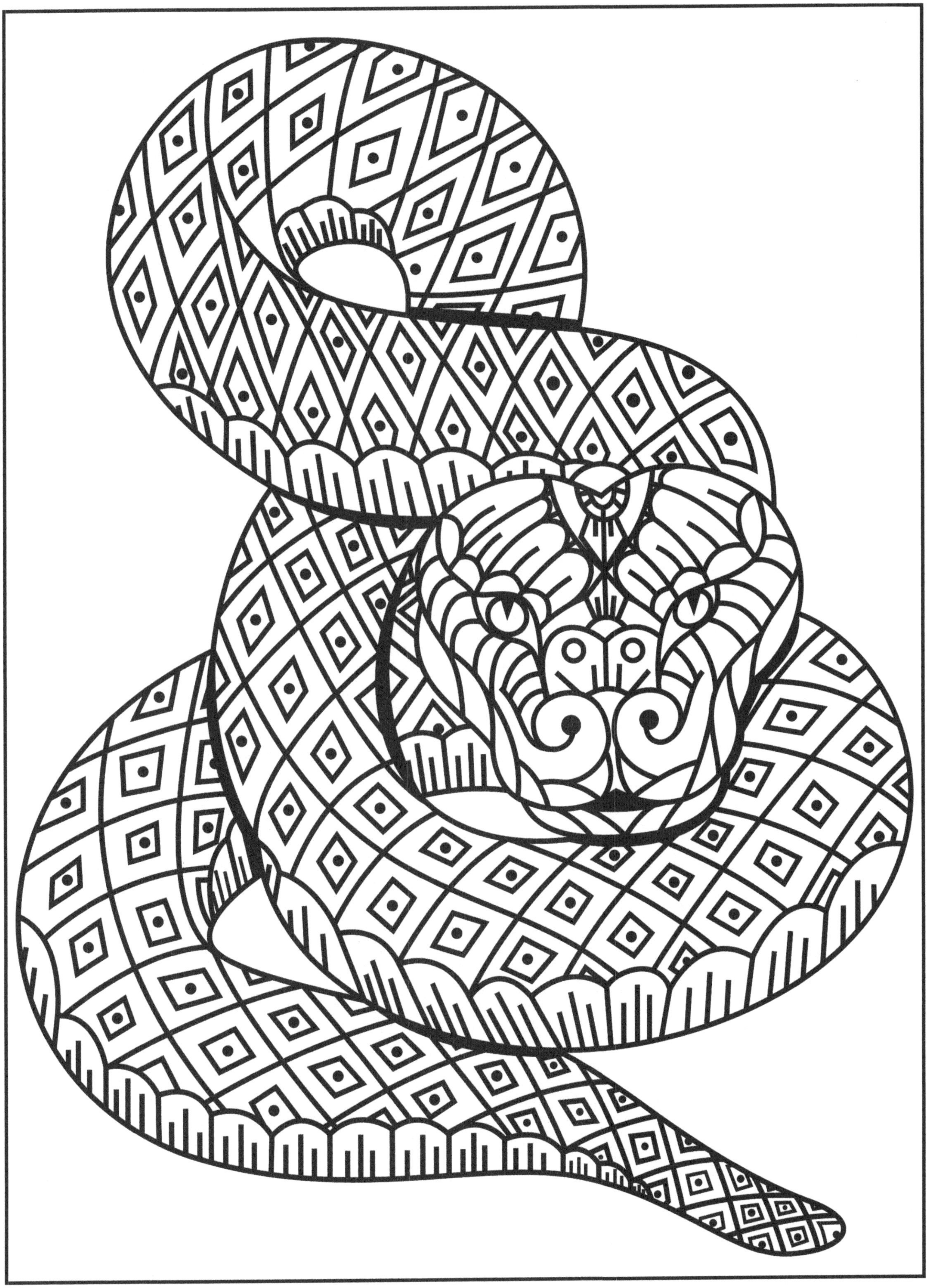

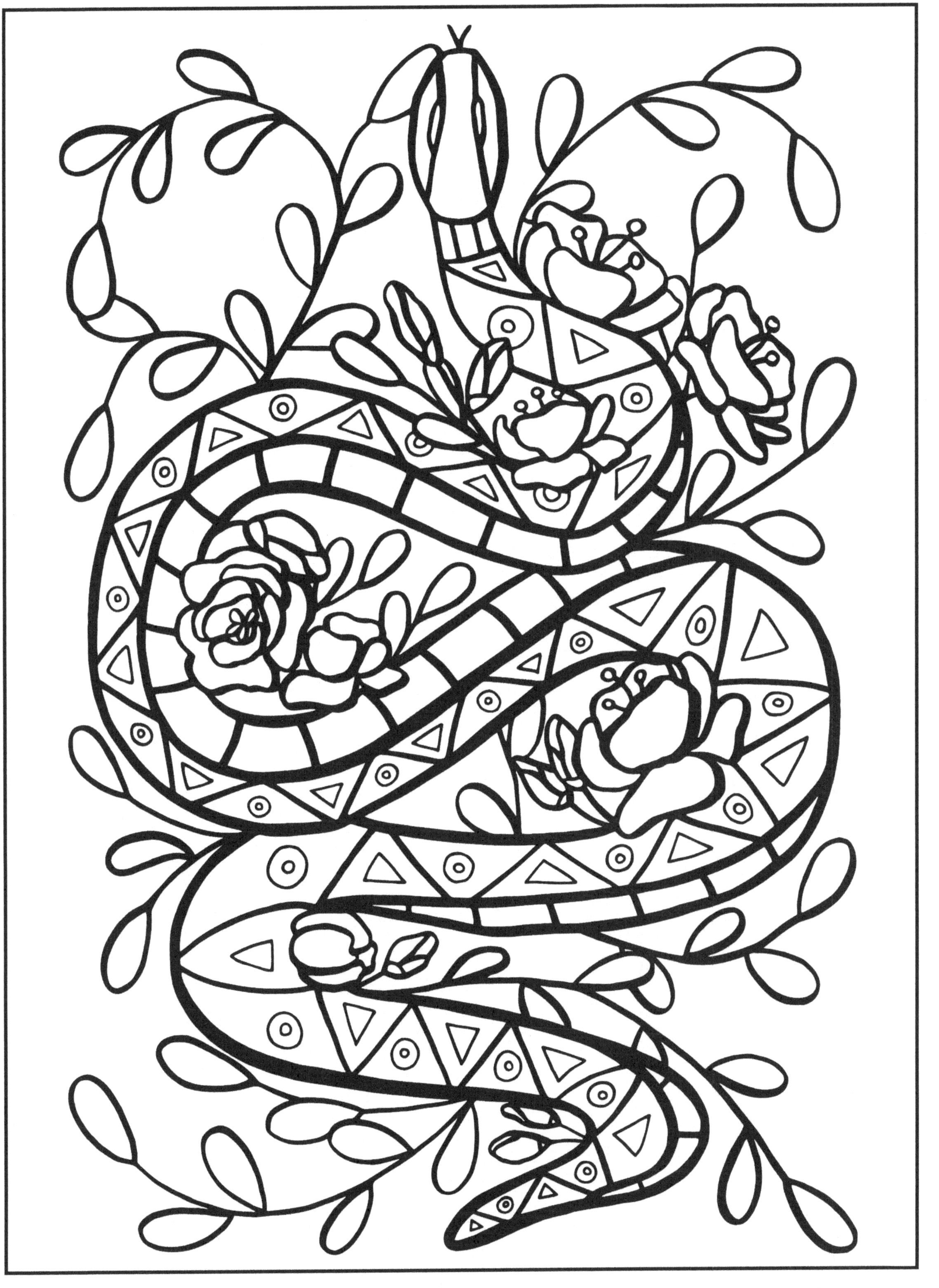

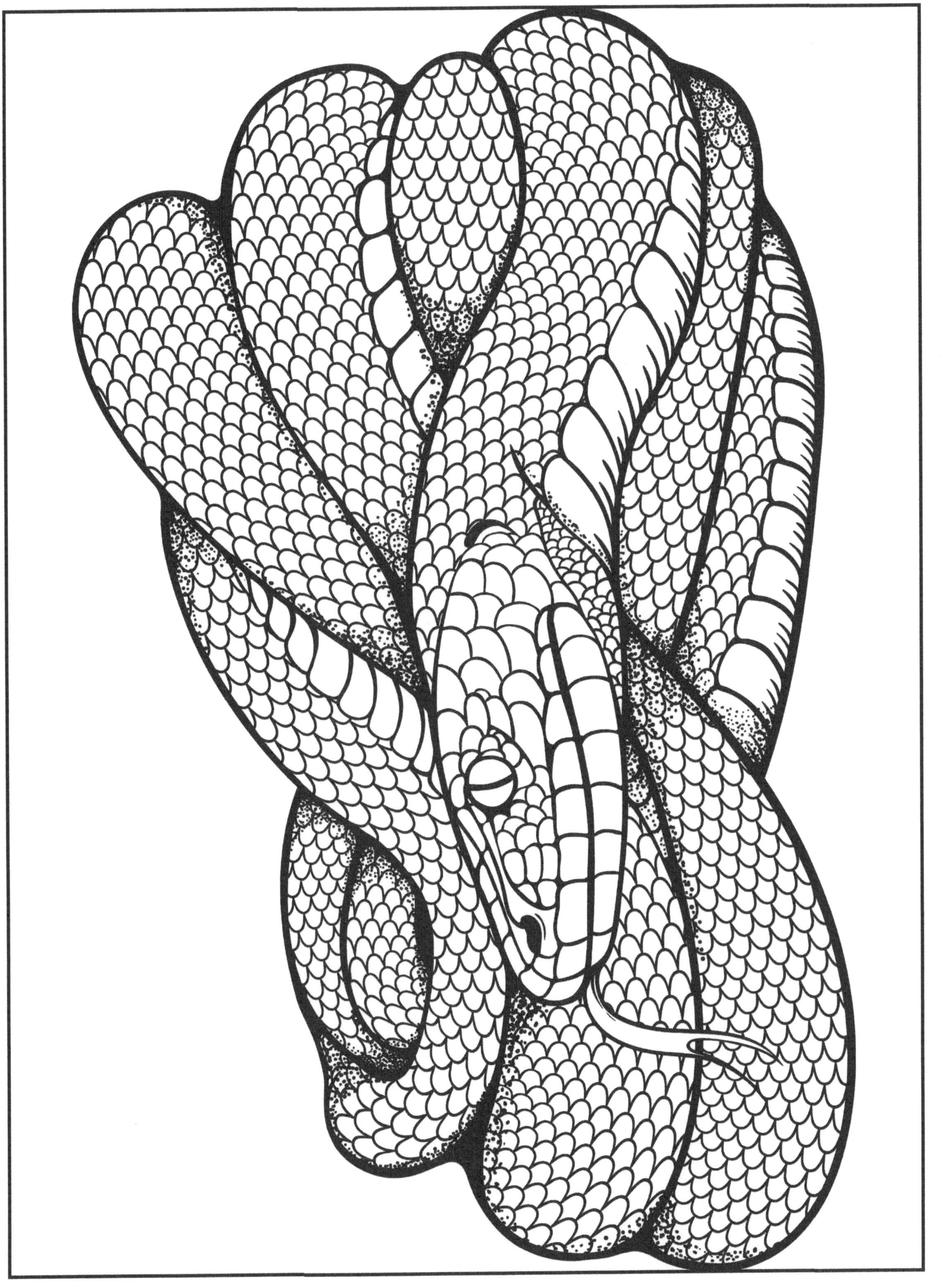

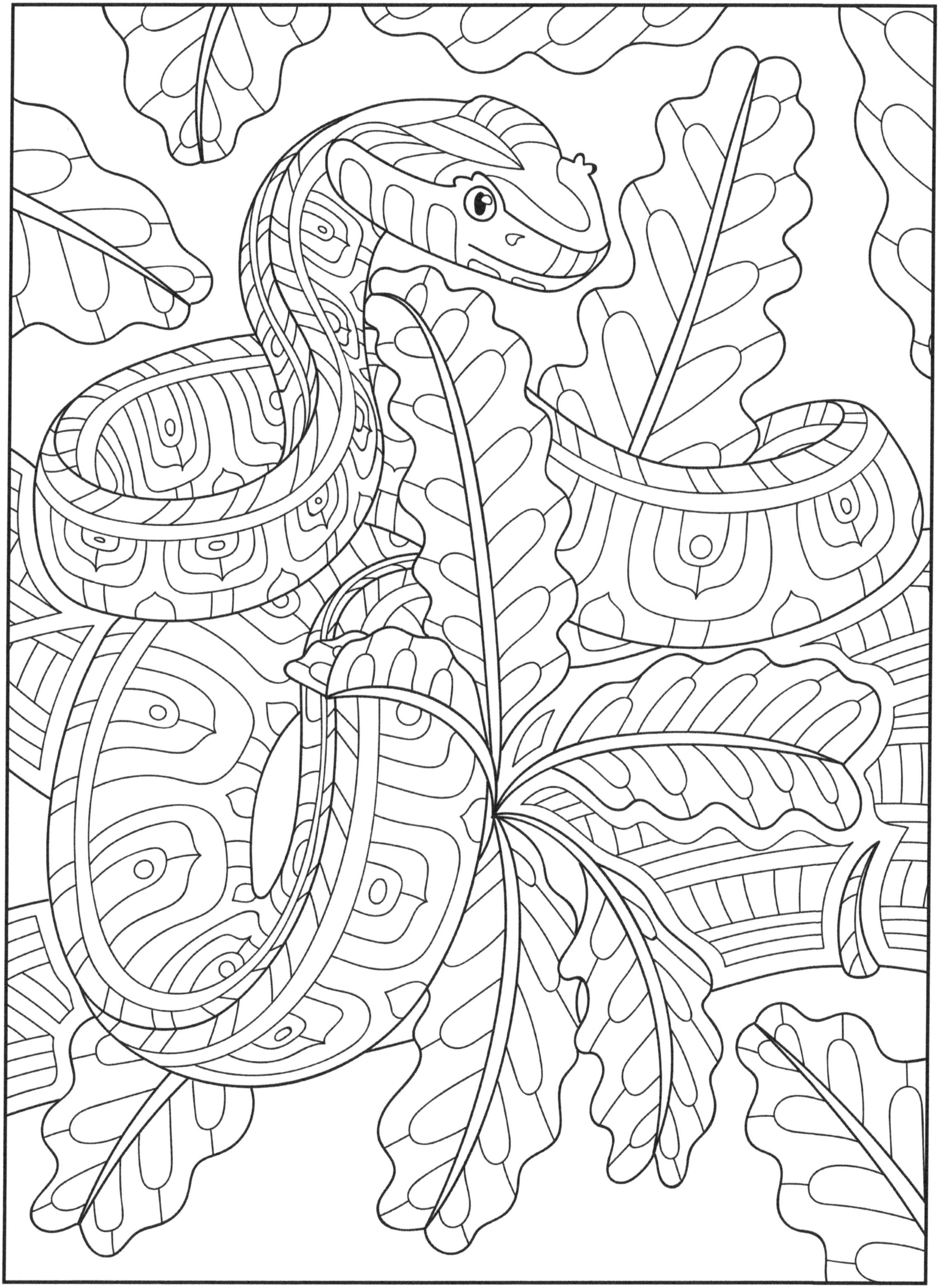

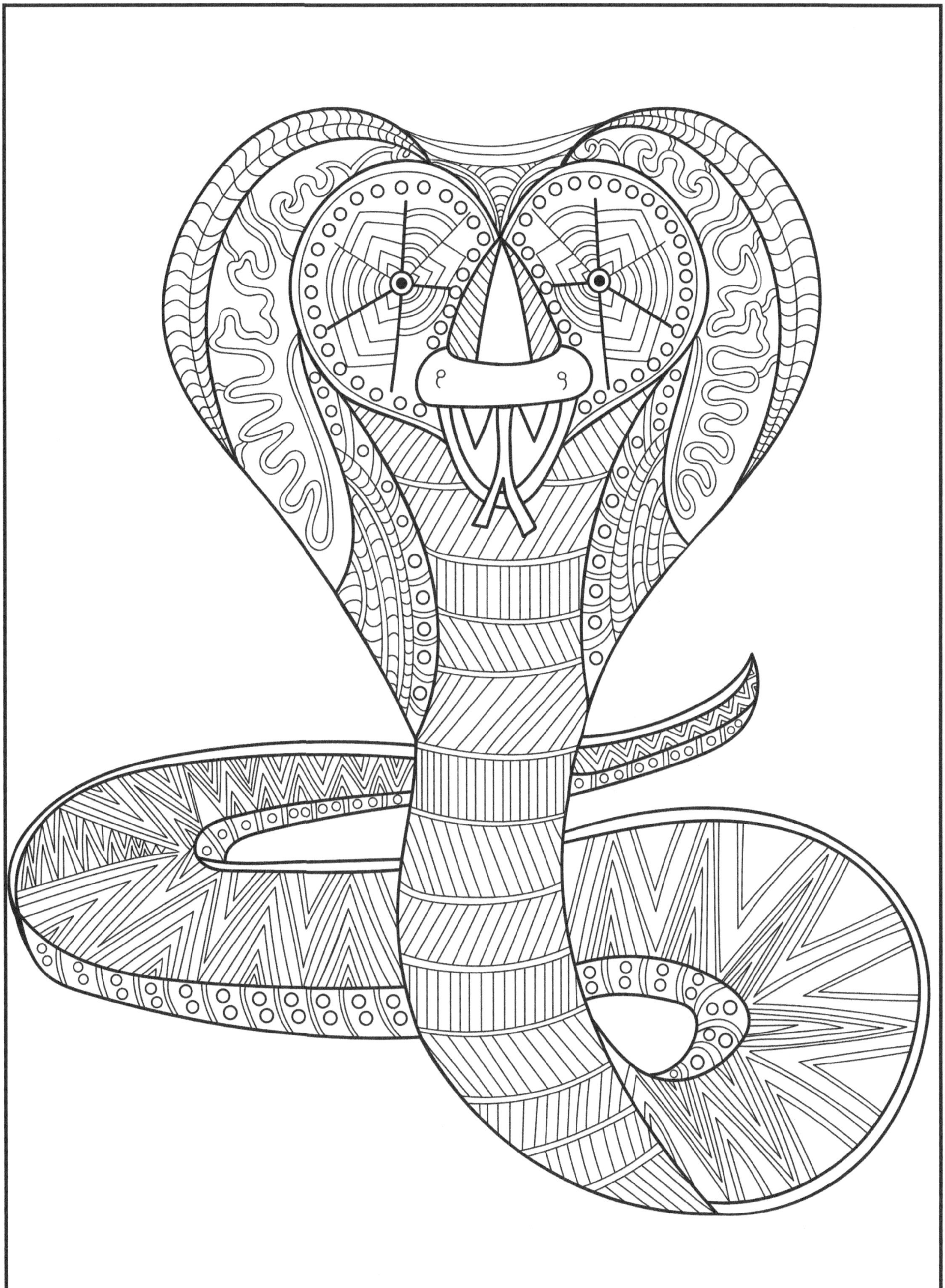

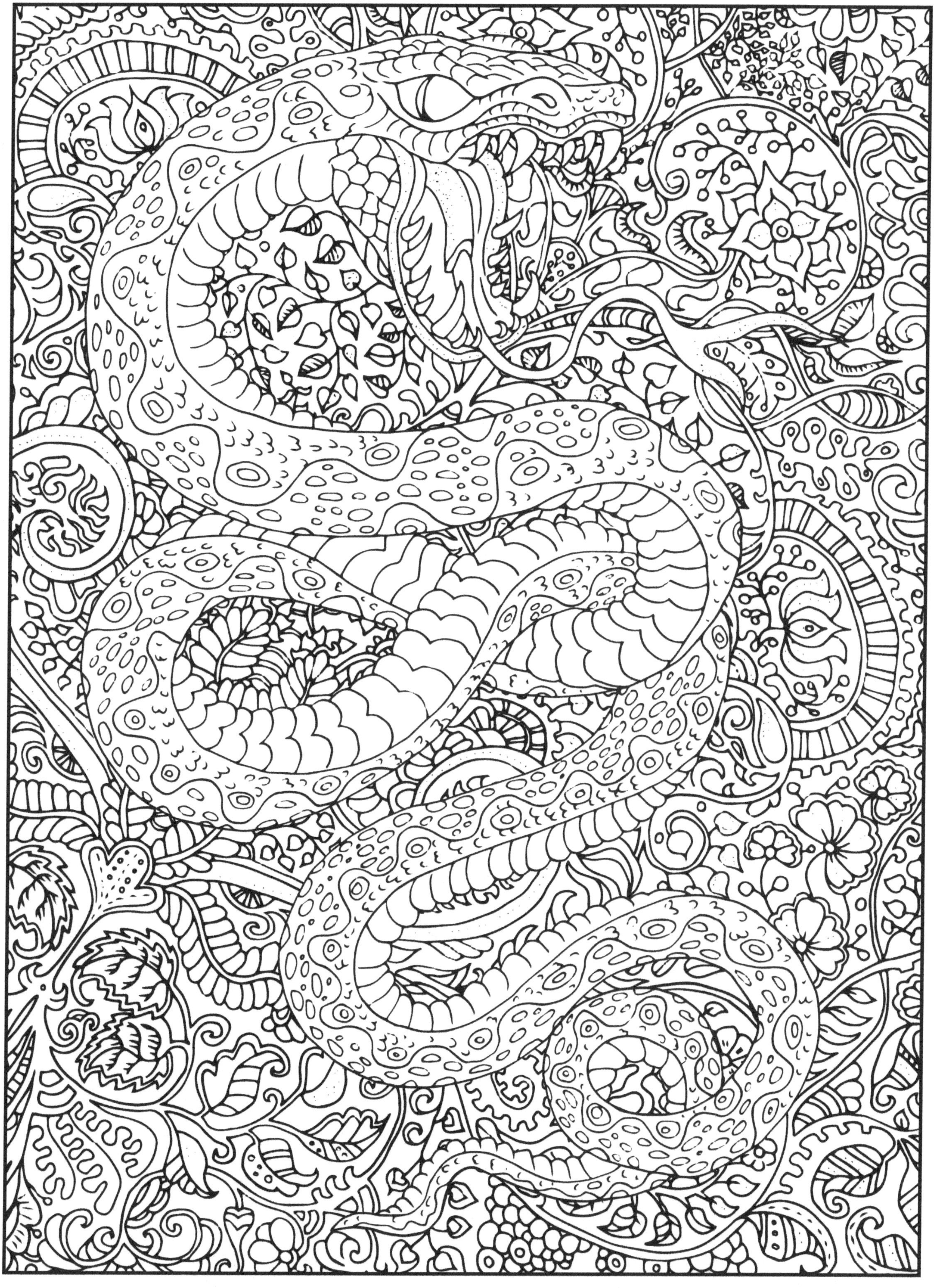

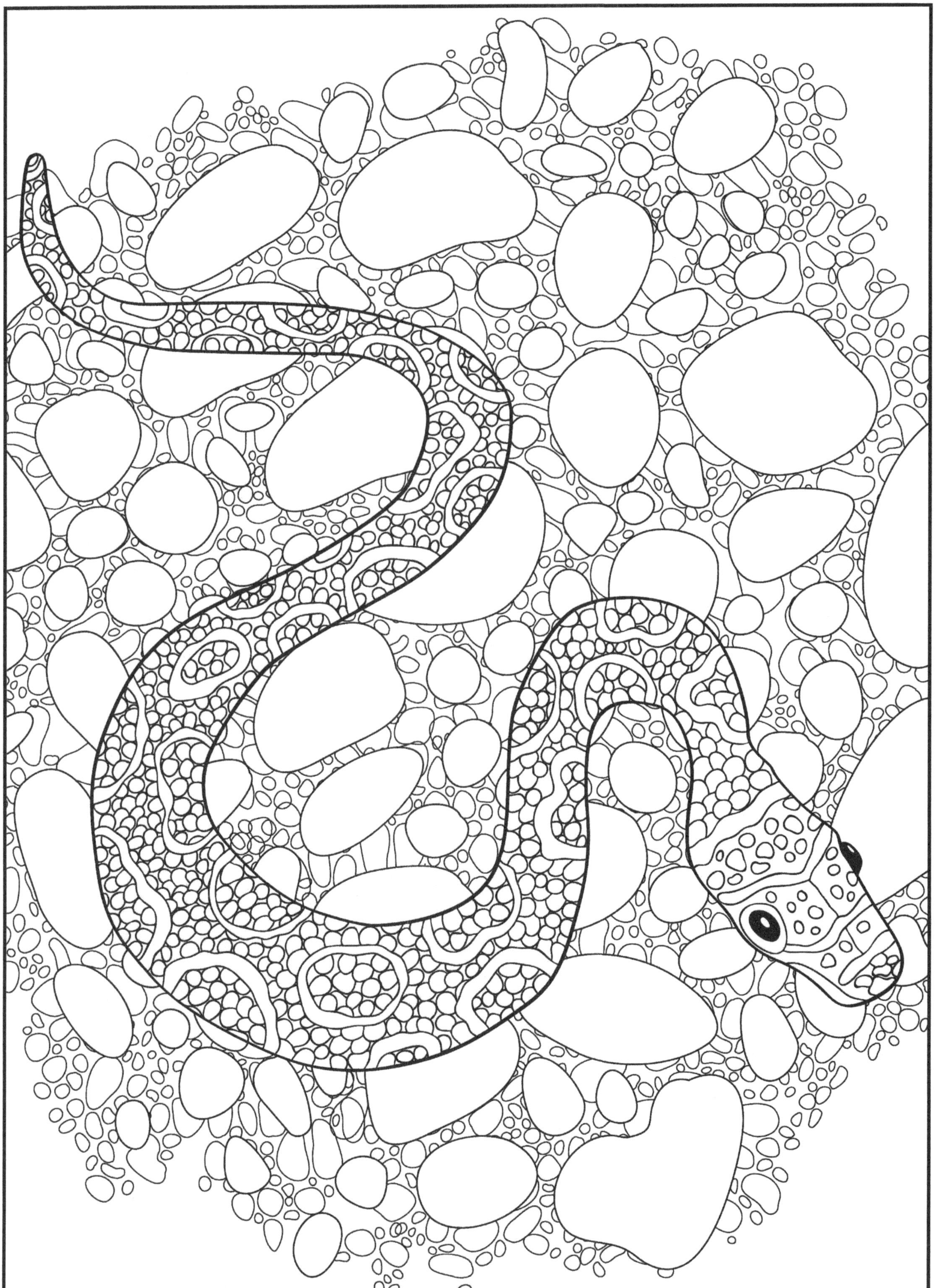

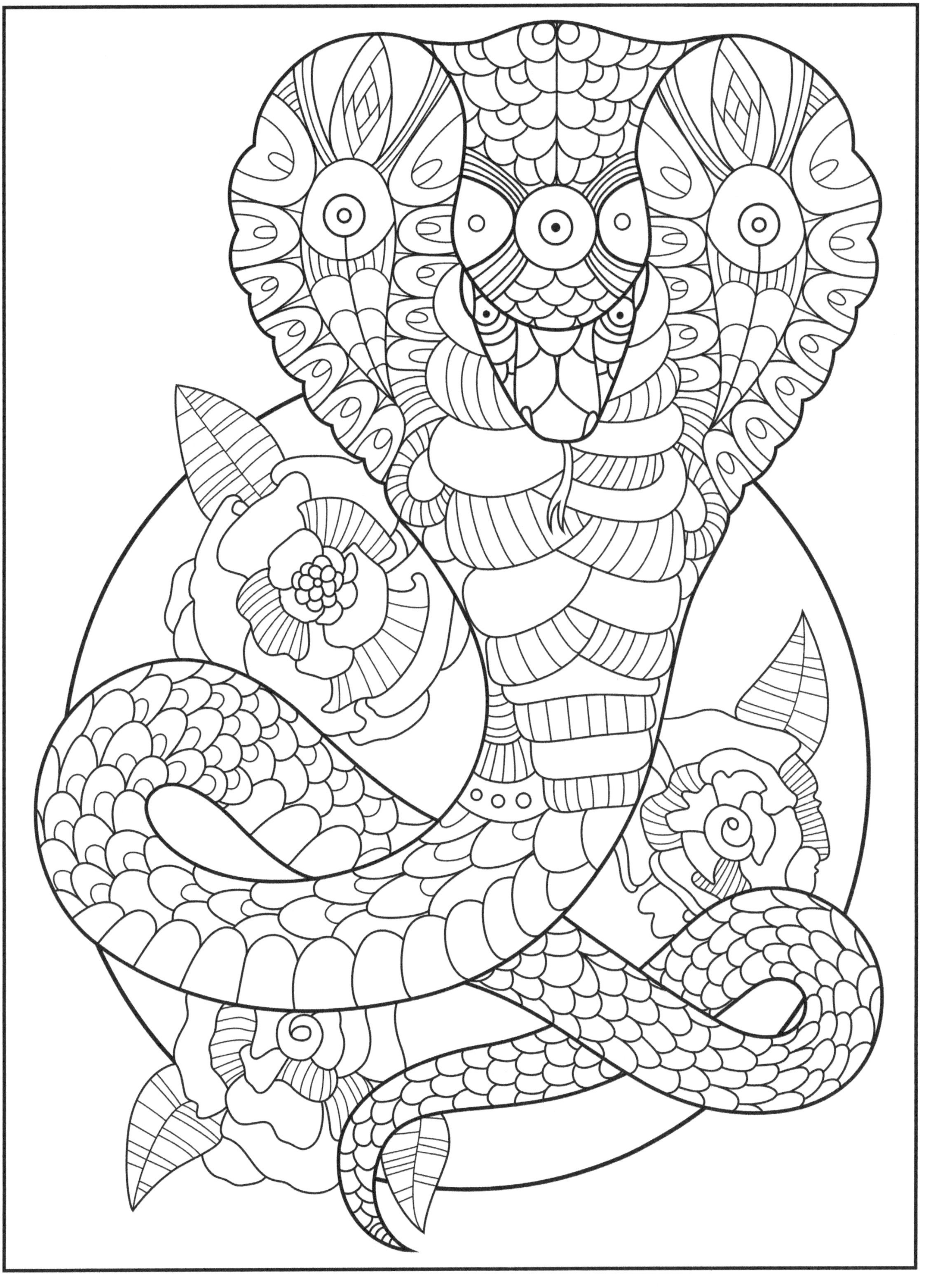

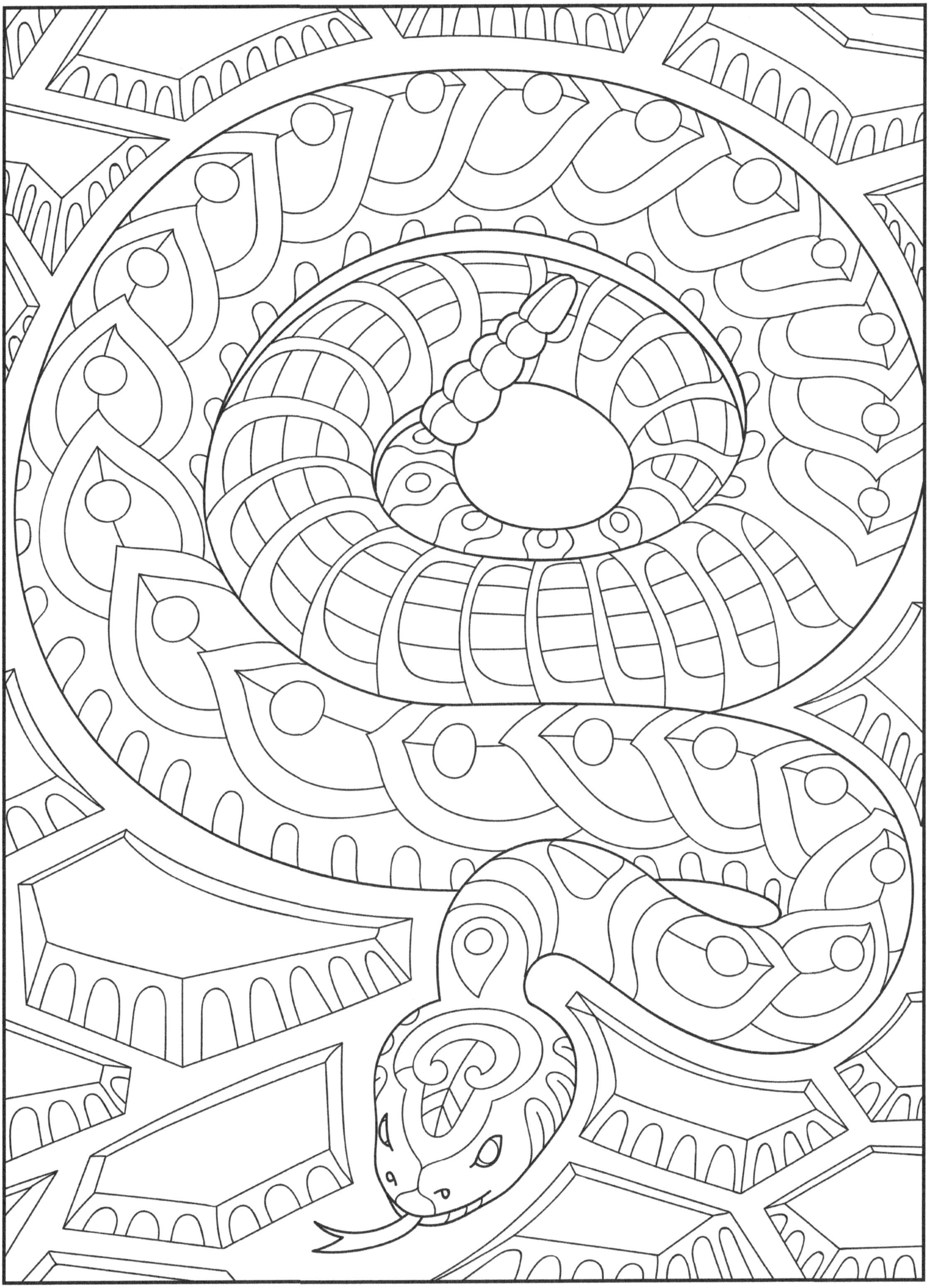

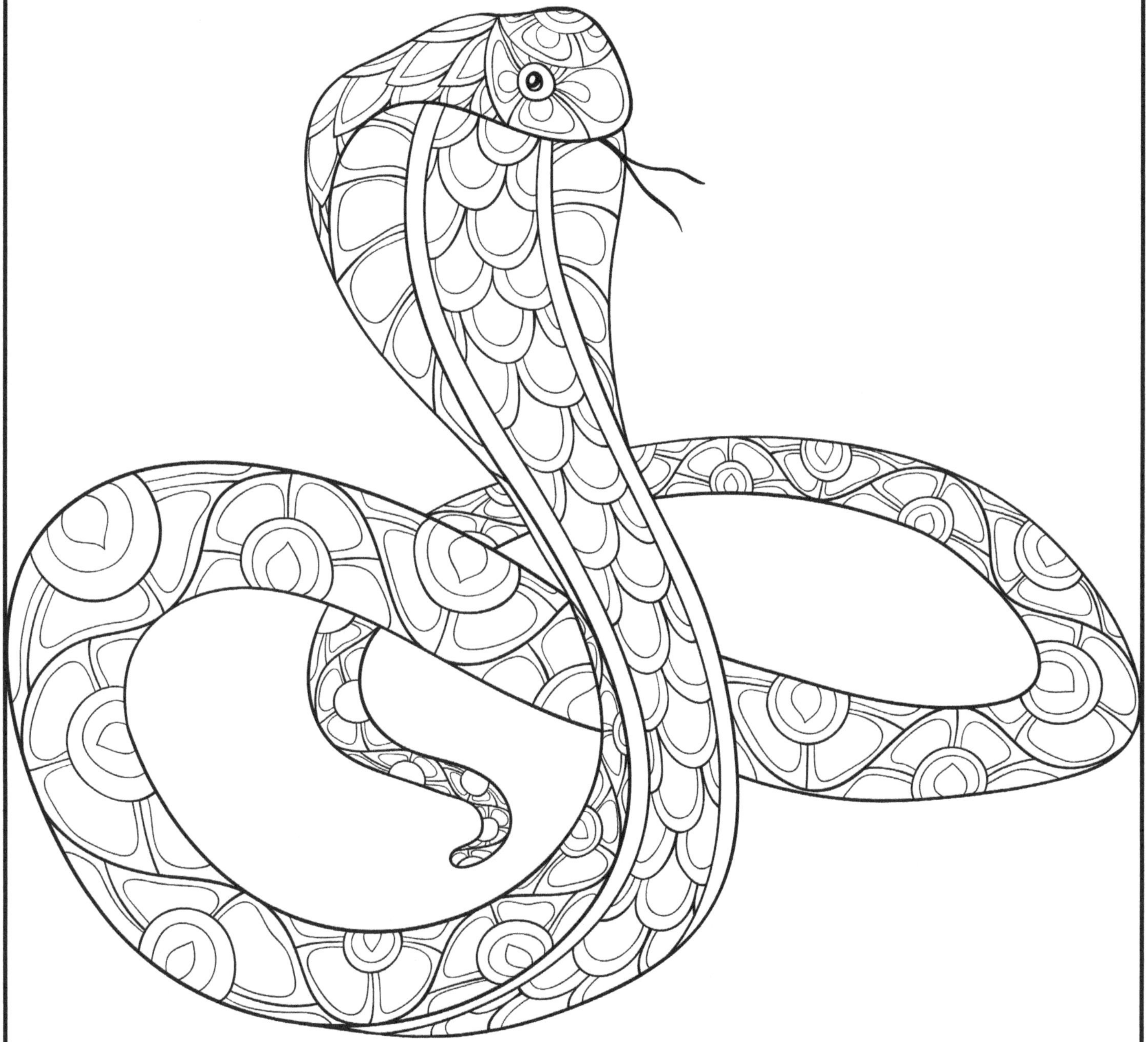

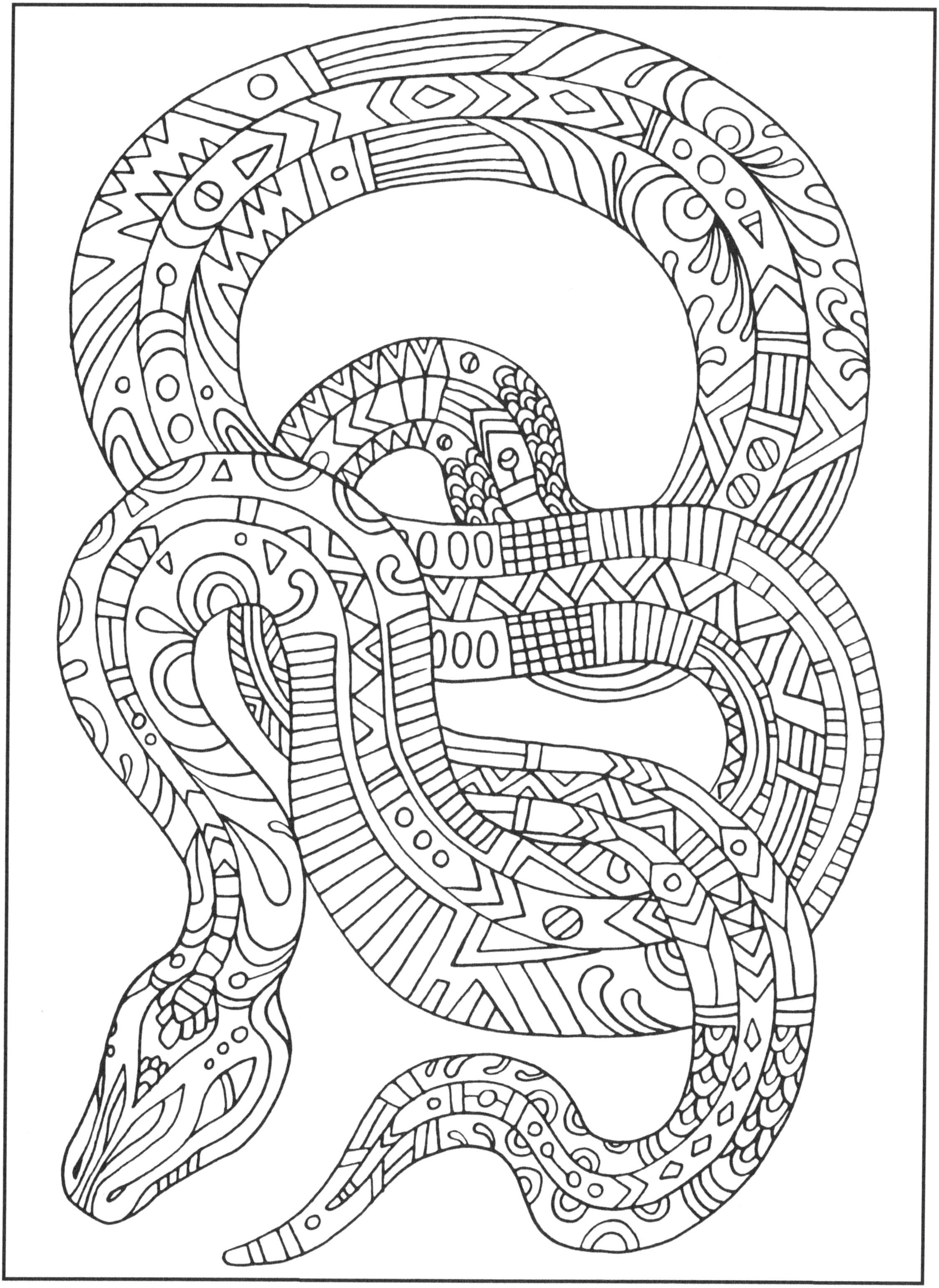

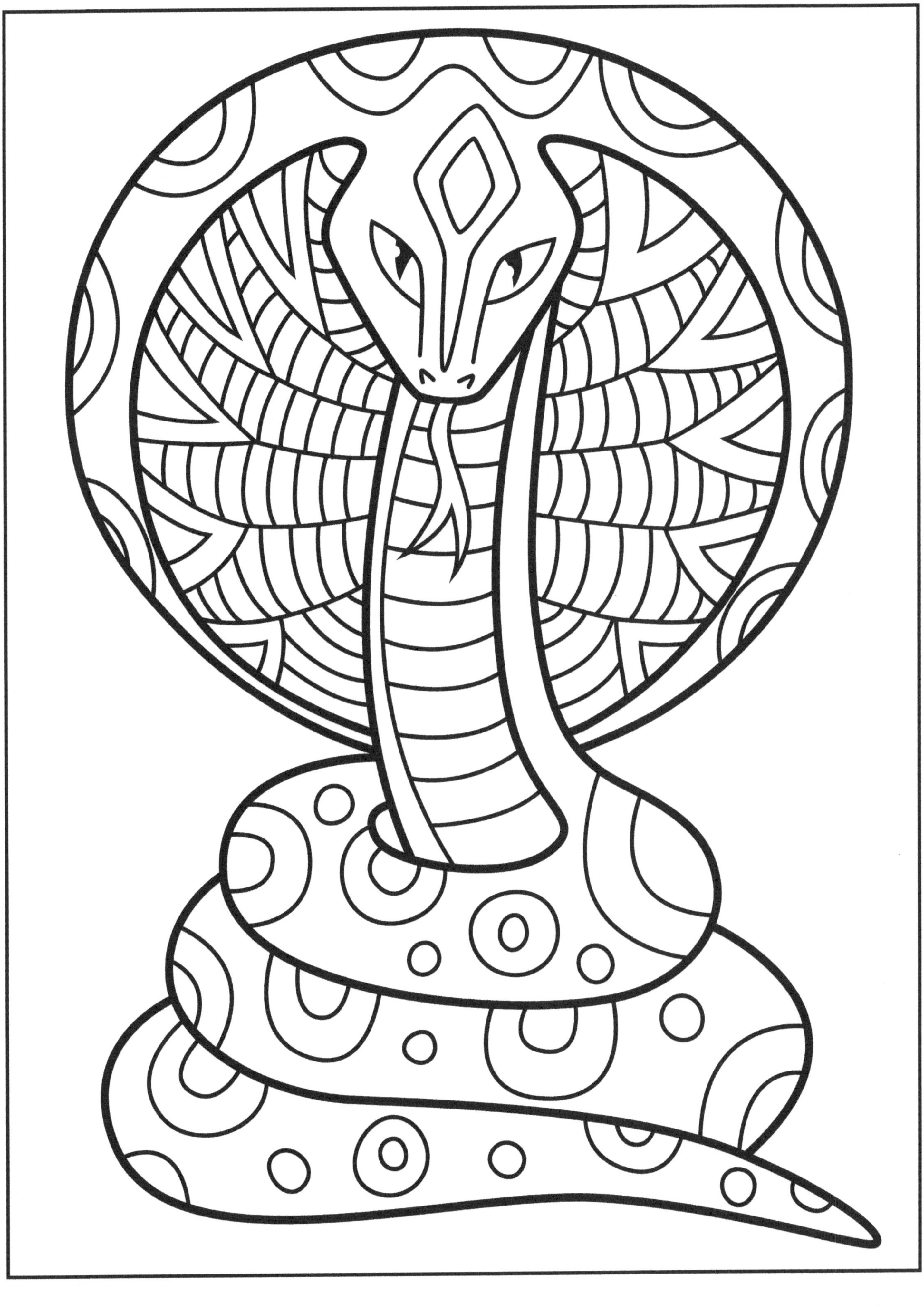

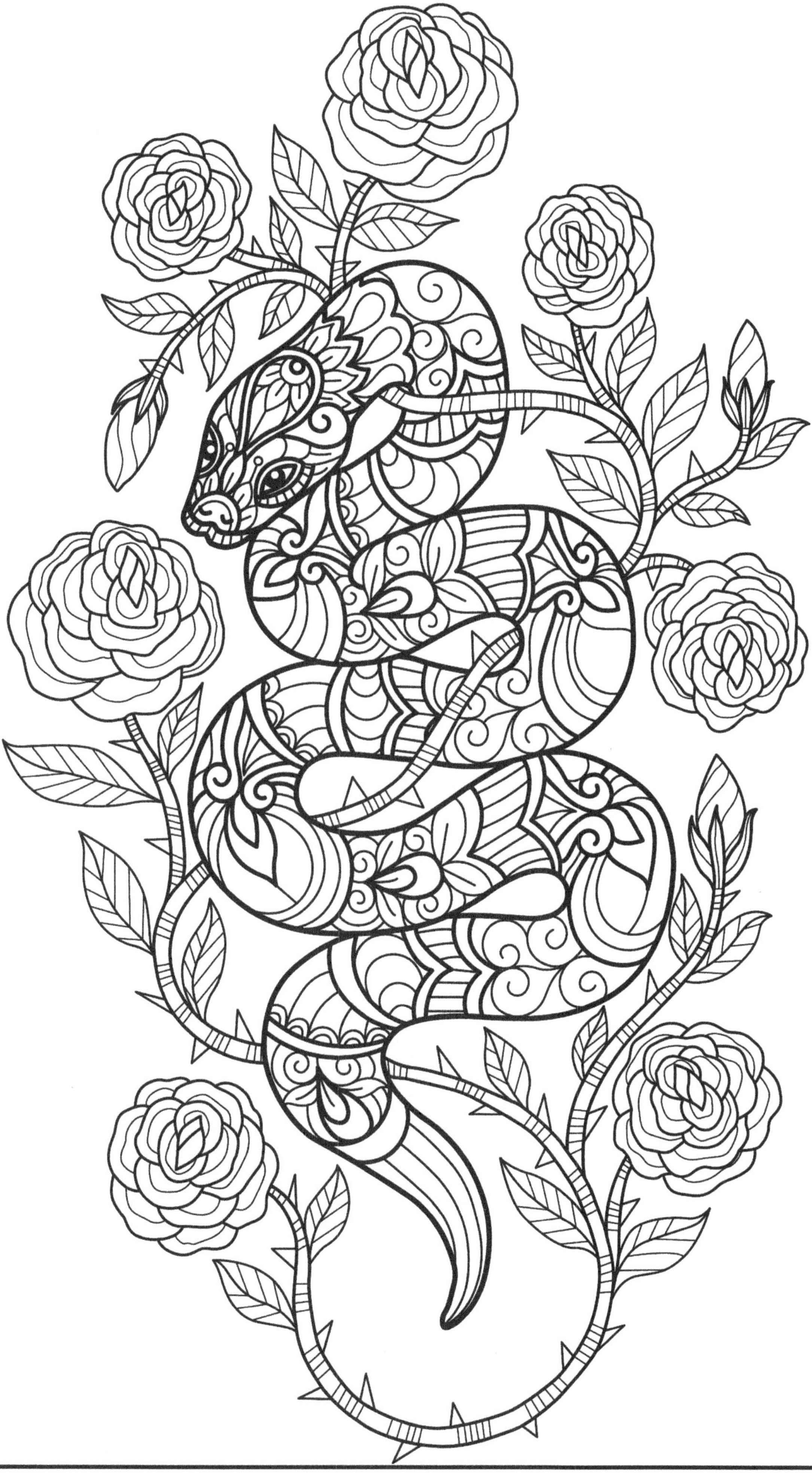

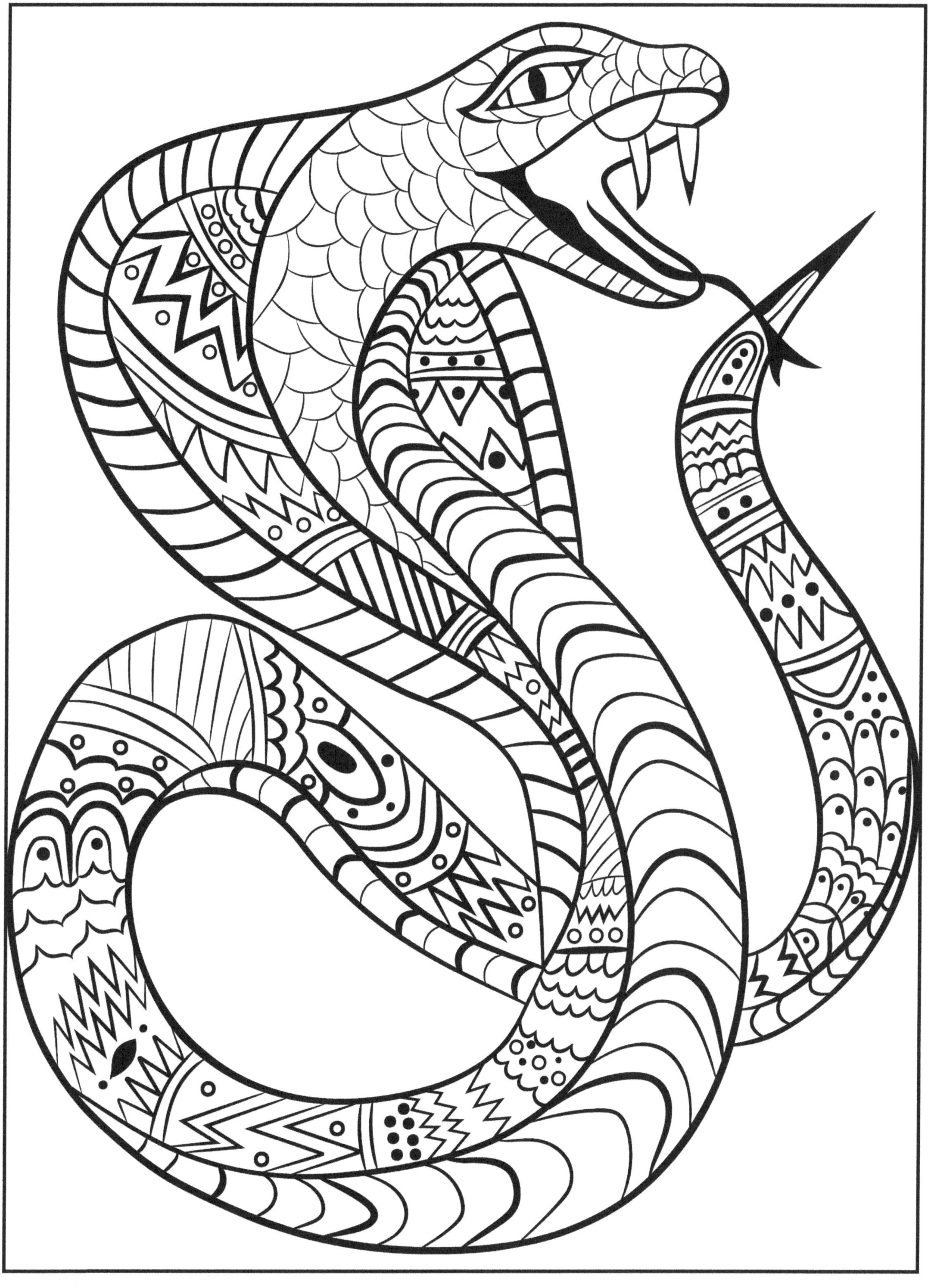

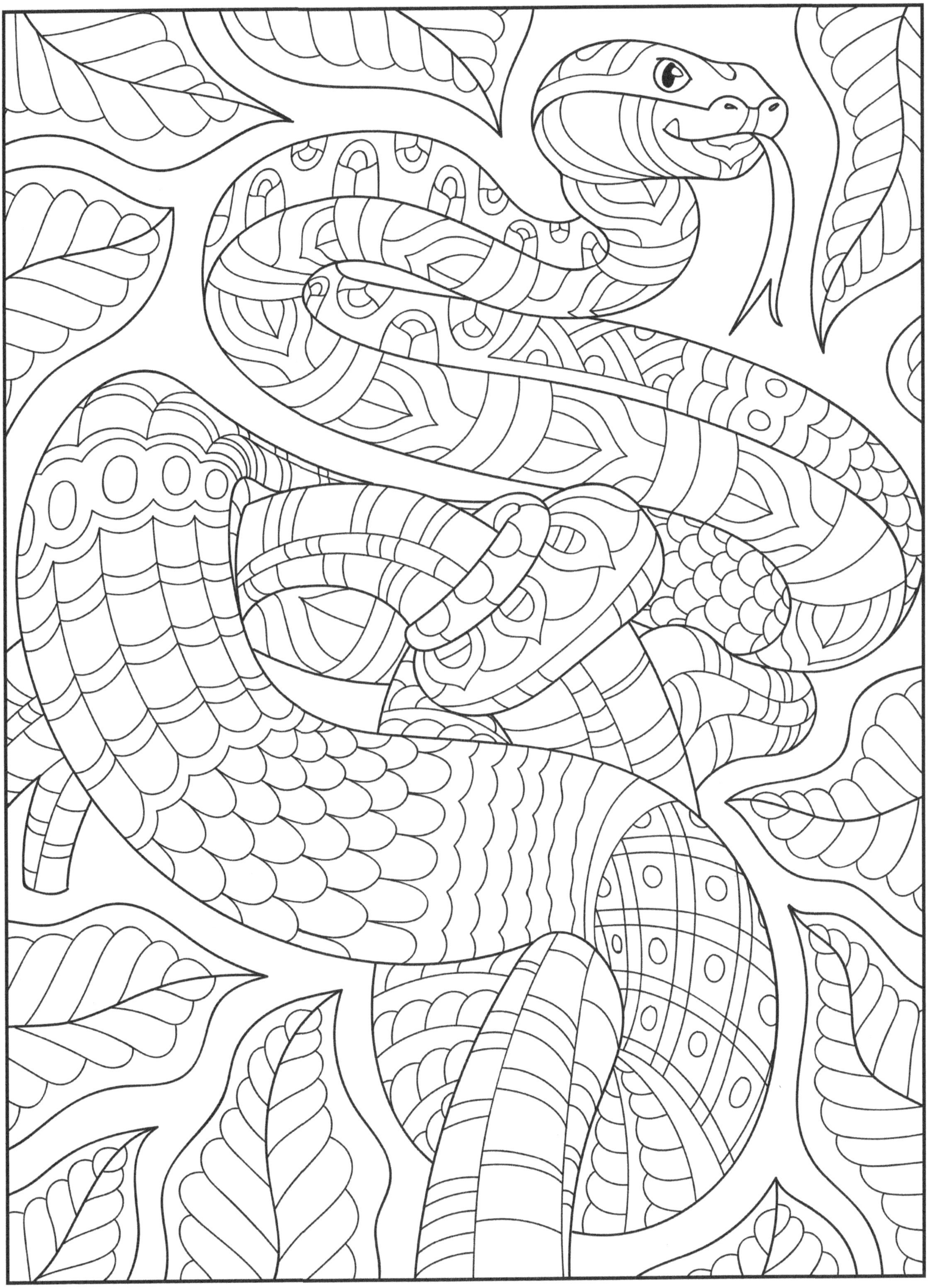

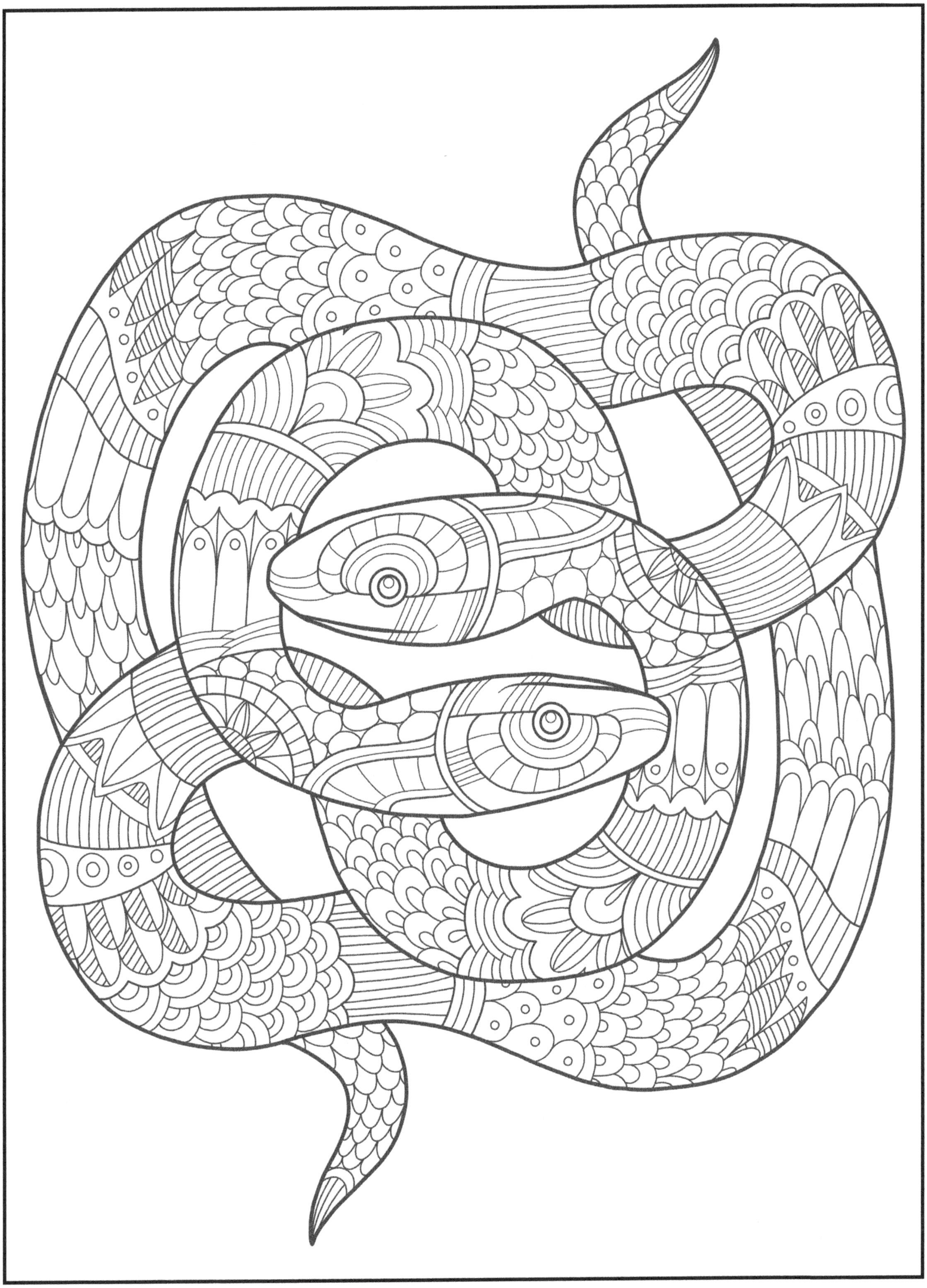

Made in the USA
Middletown, DE
24 March 2023

27574928R00044